Christine J. Cook

THE **STENCIL** BOOK

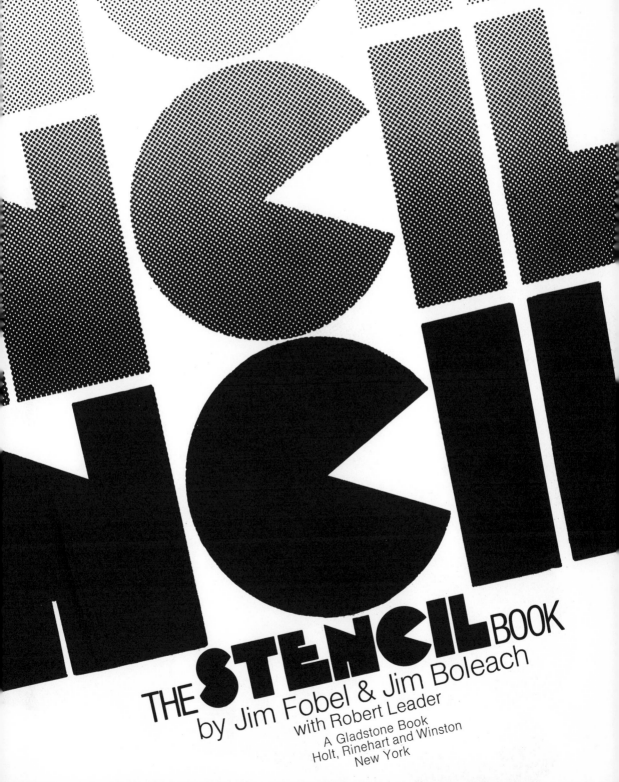

THE STENCIL BOOK

by Jim Fobel & Jim Boleach
with Robert Leader

A Gladstone Book
Holt, Rinehart and Winston
New York

For Maxine and Airi, with love

Illustrations by Miki
Special photography by John Garetti
Nefertiti Notecard designed by Rowann Gilman, Seventeen
Amerindian Matchstick Blind designed by Wayne Burkey

Published simultaneously in Canada by Holt, Rinehart and Winston
of Canada, Limited.

Library of Congress Cataloging in Publication Data
Fobel, Jim.
  The stencil book.
  "A Gladstone book."
  1. Stencils and stencil cutting. I. Boleach, Jim,
joint author. II. Leader, Robert, joint author.
III. Title.
TT270.F6   745.7'3   75-21473
ISBN 0-03-089813-7

Printed in the United States of America
10 9 8 7 6 5 4 3 2 1

First Edition

Contents

Preface/ 6

Introduction: A Stenciling Primer/ 11
Preparing the Design/13
Cutting the Stencil/16
Stenciling the Object/19
Protecting the Design/27
Miscellaneous Stenciling Supplies/27

Chapter 1: Fabric/ 29
Pick-of-the-Crop Cookout Coverall/30
Dressed-Up Sling Back/35
Tropical Towel/38
Olive-Branch Summer Dress/43
Monogrammed Tote/47
Lotus Blossom T-Shirt/51
Victorian Satin Sheets and Pillowcases/58

Chapter 2: Paper/ 67
Americana Pantry Labels/68
Art Nouveau Stationery and Envelopes/72
Madame Moon's Luminaries/76
Nefertiti Notecards and Envelopes/80
Every-Occasion Gift Wrap/86
Stencilman Kite/90

Chapter 3: Food/ 93
Fleur-de-Lis Loaf/94
Well-Dressed Turkey/105
Picture-Perfect Pie and Box/110
Message Cookies/115
Sugar-Sifted Brownies/118
Celebration Cake/121
Garden Party Sandwiches/125
Fiesta Chili Pie/128

Chapter 4: Wood/ 133
Decorative Chopping Block/134
Sporty Spare Chair/137
Planned Illusion Table/142
Early American Hardwood Floor/148
Water Lily Treasure Box/153
Pine Plank Placemats/157
Amerindian Matchstick Blind/160

Chapter 5: Mixed Media/ 165
Dutch Girl Serving Tray/166
Old-Fashioned Tea Rose Trunk/169
Art Deco Auto/175
Mediterranean Floor Tiles/179
Heavenly Huge Hopscotch/184
Colonial Coal Scuttle/188
Country Floral Wall/192

A Design Collection/ 197

Preface

Stenciling is a wonderful, versatile craft—a craft that at first impressed us, then amazed us, and eventually sent us off on many crazy adventures. Although it's one of the oldest craft techniques known, stenciling—the art of cutting a design into a thin sheet of material and then applying color through the cutout—has been thoroughly modernized by new materials and methods.

Although traditional stencil materials, such as oiled paper, metal, and wood, are still useful in specific instances, we've found that newly developed materials, such as commercially prepared stencil paper or plastic acetate, are perfect for almost any project. Using waxed stencil paper, readily available in art and craft stores, you can quickly and easily cut a stencil for almost any design. And once the stencil has been cut, you can decorate just about anything, repeating and varying the design over and over.

Almost any thin, flat material can be used to make a stencil, but there are also many "found" items that can be used as stencils in their natural state. Chances are, in fact, that the very first stencils occurred naturally—a discovery of a group of missionaries to Fiji in the last century. Here's how we imagine it:

The Fiji islands, sometime in the 1800s. Scene: EXTERIOR, a wild, stormy night during the monsoon season. CUT TO: INTERIOR, a group of gaunt missionaries huddled together, praying by the light of a single hurricane lantern. Moona, a native girl, rushes in to tell her mistress, Evangeline, that Evangeline's young son has wandered into the storm. Evangeline throws a shawl around her shoulders and, ignoring the protests of her friends, rushes blindly into the night. For hours she runs through the tangled jungle, her cries drowned out by the shriek of the wind and the roar of the rain. Exhausted, she stumbles into a clearing and faints in front of a tiny hut. Two withered brown hands reach to lift her as the scene DISSOLVES TO:

The INTERIOR of the hut. It is morning, and the sun shines brightly through the woven slats of the walls. Evangeline wakes with a start, looks wildly about the room, and sinks back to the mat. Her clothes have been draped near a small fire to dry. She looks down at her body and is surprised to find that she's enveloped in layers of beautifully decorated cloth, the likes of which she has never seen. As she examines the brightly colored abstract designs, her face lights up in inspiration.

Perhaps the desperate financial situation of the tiny island community can be solved (there has recently been an outbreak of plague and a hospital is urgently needed) by exporting this native cloth back to England. Shielded by her exotic blankets, she tentatively emerges from the hut.

In the clearing, sitting in the sun and stenciling a length of tapa cloth, is an ancient island woman. Evangeline, eyes shining with gratitude, silently sits beside the woman and watches her as she works.

As the woman's deft hands rapidly apply color through the banana leaf stencils, she begins to speak in halting English of the origin of stenciling. A gift from the gods, she says, given when the world was young. The gods sent a worm into the jungle with instructions to burrow into the new, tightly curled leaves of the banana tree. As the leaves unfurled, they revealed a series of small, oddly shaped holes, perfectly graduated from large to small. When the leaves were placed on cloth and color applied, the result was a brilliant, intricate design. And the gods were pleased to see their children clothed so beautifully.

"So am I," gushes Evangeline. She rushes back to the settlement— finding her son on the way—to proclaim the glad tidings, and the story ends very, very happily.

Without the Hollywood embellishments, the story is basically true. The development of stenciling on isolated South Sea islands is only one piece of evidence that suggests the craft may have been employed in decorative processes long before the beginnings of recorded history.

There is argument as to whether the Egyptians did or did not use stencils to reproduce hieroglyphics some five thousand years ago, but there is no doubt that stencils were used by the ancient Chinese. One of the oldest examples of stenciling is to be found in China in the almost inaccessible Caves of a Thousand Buddhas, where the walls and ceilings are covered with—not surprisingly—thousands of stenciled images of Buddha. The particular religious sect that maintained these caves had the notion that every time they painted the master's face, they themselves moved a little closer to Buddhahood. Being wondrously inventive, they used stenciling to speed the process.

Even though much knowledge and many art forms were lost during the Dark Ages, stenciling somehow survived. In the Middle East, stencils were used to decorate luxurious silks and to illuminate manuscripts with delicate designs. Unlettered monarchs of the Middle Ages, such as Emperor Justinian and King Theodoric, used golden stencils to affix their initials to official documents rather than sign with the proverbial X. (Even with a stencil, poor Justinian needed someone to guide his hand.)

In France, during the late Middle Ages and early Renaissance, craftsmen used stencils to produce playing cards in such large quantities that furtive card games posed a threat to the country's productivity, causing the issue of several stern edicts. It was also in France that craftsmen used stencils to make the first flocked wallpaper; they applied size, a sticky substance, through stencil openings and then blew shredded wool onto the gluey design. Stenciling was, in fact, enormously popular in France, more than in any other European country. One Frenchman was so renowned for his stencil designs that he was officially exempted from paying taxes!

Thousands of miles away, the Japanese were creating some of the most beautiful stencils ever made and using them to decorate silk clothing and screens. To make their intricate, delicate stencils, Japanese artists used paper made of pressed mulberry fiber and waterproofed with persimmon juice. The long, painstaking process involved making two identical stencils, reinforcing them with a fine web of human hair, and gluing them together.

In colonial America, itinerant stencilers wandered the countryside in search of employment. Because European carpets and wallpaper were prohibitively expensive, these artisans used stencils to decorate floors with carpet designs and walls with floral designs and geometric borders. Many examples of the work of these craftsmen, who usually lived-in with the families they were working for, have been preserved and can be seen today. Some stencilers—Moses Eaton, for example—developed such distinctive styles that their work is recognizable at a glance.

By the 1800s, the craft of stenciling had expanded beyond walls and floors, and a number of factories were using stencils to decorate other household items. It was such a factory in Connecticut that offered one of the first opportunities for women to hang up their aprons and work outside the home.

Stenciling continued to be an important industrial process for repeating decorative designs until the early part of this century, when silk screening was developed. As the silk-screening process was refined, the age-old craft of stenciling began to be relegated to utilitarian uses such as sign-making, lettering, and numbering.

There were, however, a few exceptions to these mundane uses. During the 1940s, there appeared a particular brand of exotic imagery that depended upon stencils for its slick illustrative characteristics. The artists who promoted this specialized look used air-brushes to spray fine mists of color through stencils to achieve a consistent commercial quality for subjects that always seemed to include parrots, cockatoos, and flamingos; still lifes of orchids, gardenias, and magnolia blossoms; lots of palm trees and tropical vegetation; and, of course, shoulder-padded, be-wedgied women wearing strange-looking hats.

But these bursts of stenciled imagery were rare and confined to specialized industries and small groups of artists. Very little in the way of materials existed for the individual who wished to practice the craft. For years, the only precut stencils generally available were the ordinary cardboard letter stencils that most of us used as children and teen-agers to decorate notebooks, signs, and school projects. Recently, however, interest in stenciling has begun to grow by leaps and bounds.

We first realized the versatility of stencils several years ago. At that time we owned a company called the Picture Pie Company, originated to promote the concept of Edible Art. Our first products were pies, each handpainted with brilliantly colored designs. Customers could order whatever they wanted on a pie top—portraits, landscapes, still lifes—and we would painstakingly paint the image with special food colors. Because of the amount of labor involved, prices ranged from $25 to $250. Despite the high prices, the pies were a success, and we began to produce other food items: shaped breads with handpainted messages, painted cookies, and fully dressed turkeys (one of the projects in this book).

When a major Manhattan department store offered us a third of its bake shop from which to operate, what had started as a small, custom art form suddenly became a monster of a business that began to consume us.

One of our major problems was that there just wasn't enough time to physically paint all the food items on order. One day, after several abortive attempts at assembly-line art, inspiration, like the light bulb in comic strips, flashed. We had a solution: stencils. We cut waxed paper stencils, placed them over the pastry dough, and voila! a perfect design every time.

Stenciling freed us from so much time-consuming labor and supervision that we were able to go on to even greater culinary masterpieces, such as the dinner we catered for a Park Avenue grande dame. We first had a friend construct a small park bench out of clay. Then we wired three roasting chickens to the bench in sitting positions, wings on hips and drumsticks crossed. We adorned the naked chickens with pastry clothing, handbags, and shoes, all of which had been stenciled with tiny prints. After baking them, we attached blond-haired, elaborately coiffured dolls' heads. Our silly chicken ladies were then placed on the dining table along with bonsai trees and an oval pie that was painted blue and ornamented with ceramic ducks and swans.

Soon after this festive meal, stenciling landed us in a lot of trouble. As a joke, someone suggested we create a line of "status breads," copying the designs of the expensive handbags carried by so many Manhattan women. We made a few loaves of bread shaped like clutch bags and put them in the shop's window. We were amazed at the number of laughing shoppers who wheeled through the revolving door to stand in line to buy a status loaf. We chuckled along with them.

Two weeks after a well-known columnist published a humorous story about our company and featured a photo of one of our loaves, which happened to carry a somewhat irreverent takeoff on the name of a famous handbag designer, the laughter stopped. We received a fat sheaf of legal papers informing us we were being sued for a million dollars. We sent the offended bag man a hundred Good Humor bars, hoping his heart would melt along with them, but to no avail. Eventually, the lawsuit was dropped because of a technicality, but the whole situation was half-baked, unkneaded, and simply incrEDIBLE; the moral being: Stencil wisely.

As we cut stencils for the picture pies, we began to see just how versatile stencils are. Though the stencils we were using were designed to decorate baked goods, we knew that the same stencils could be used on a number of surfaces. It also became apparent that there was almost a total lack of precut stencils on the market. After disbanding the Picture Pie Company and forming another, we began to manufacture precut stencil kits.

Though we found a few books on the subject of stenciling, we discovered that most of them either were hopelessly outdated or had completely ignored the abundance of new materials that makes stenciling easier, faster, and more permanent. We saw a need for a comprehensive book that would not only explain simply and completely how to make custom stencils but would also generate an awareness of the infinite uses of stencils.

Almost any surface can be stenciled upon, using the proper coloring tool and the correct applicator. Once you know the proper methods and materials, it's simply a matter of selecting a design, transferring the design, cutting the stencil, and then stenciling whatever object you wish. Each of the steps is an easy process—cutting a stencil, for example, is much easier than drawing a straight line. And once you've cut a stencil, it can be used to decorate walls, floors, clothing, furniture, stationery, giftwrap, cookies, cakes; in short, just about anything. (You could even use a stencil to apply a pair of perfectly arched eyebrows.)

Not only is stenciling one of the simplest and most inexpensive crafts, it's also a craft that lets you see immediate results. Once you've experimented and have become familiar with the basics (and it doesn't take long), you'll be amazed at how quickly you can stencil. And, unlike many crafts, stenciling can be molded to fit your personal schedule. You can quickly spray-paint a box top for instant gift wrap or take your time stenciling a design on a piece of furniture, savoring the tranquillity that this craft can bring.

It has been a joy and a pleasure writing this book. We have included all the hints that space would permit and have tried to create a wide range of design styles for you to choose from: early American, floral, Oriental, Egyptian, Arts Deco and Nouveau, contemporary, American Indian, and several images designed specially to appeal to children. If you save the stencils you cut for each project, you'll always have a collection of designs at your fingertips for instant decoration. But remember, these designs are only a beginning, and the sources of inspiration are limitless. Once you've exhausted the designs here, you'll have had enough experience to be able to translate designs, pictures, and patterns from any source into stencils.

After you've tried a few projects, you'll probably agree that the greatest thrill is the moment the stencil is ready to be removed. As it's lifted away and you suddenly see the finished design, an irrepressible feeling of pride and a sense of accomplishment will always follow. And it's this feeling, this appreciation of what your own two hands can do, that makes all handcrafting a fantastic, beautiful experience.

Introduction
A Stenciling Primer

There are three basic kinds of stencils: modular stencils, full-design stencils, and registration stencils. Although we employ each of the three types in our various projects, whenever possible we prefer to use modular stencils—stencils that are parts of a design and that make a finished design when repeated.

Modular stencils have several advantages over other types. For one thing, they save time during the cutting stage. For example, assume you wish to stencil a flower that has twelve petals. Using the modular method, you need cut only one petal and then repeat it twelve times.

You can also achieve great variety and versatility with modular stencils. If you cut a nonmodular stencil of, say, a basket of flowers, you'll be able to use the design only in the form of the stencil you've cut. But if you've divided the design into components—two different flowers, a section of the basket, a vine, several leaves—you'll not only be able to rearrange the flowers in the basket, you'll also be able to make the overall design as large or as small as you wish.

Registration Stencil

Modular Stencil

Full-Design Stencil

In some cases, modular stencils are an absolute necessity. It would be absurd, for instance, to try to cut a stencil large enough to cover an entire floor.

But one of the best reasons for using modular stencils is that they're fun. With a small collection of basic shapes—several rectangles, a heart, a squiggle or two, a teardrop, some circles—you can create an endless variety of borders, geometric designs, still lifes, and even landscapes.

Full-design stencils are those into which a complete design has been cut. These stencils can be filled in with one color, as in our Dutch Girl Tray, or several different colors, as in our Colonial Coal Scuttle, if care is taken that the color intended for one area does not overlap into an area intended for another color.

Registration stencils are often used to separate colors. If, for example, you wanted to stencil a design of red and blue, you could cut one stencil that included all the red components of the design and one that included all the blue. Each stencil and the object to be stenciled would be marked with registration marks to ensure that the completed design aligned correctly. Registration stencils can also be used to achieve a handpainted effect by eliminating, in the final design, all stencil bridges (see page 15).

No matter what type of stencil you're using, stenciling involves three steps: enlarging and/or transferring the design, cutting the stencil, and stenciling the design onto the object. In discussing these techniques and the materials and tools that can be used, we've tried to be comprehensive; don't feel that you have to run right out and buy everything we mention. For most of our projects, a few basic, inexpensive tools and materials will do nicely. Later, after you've begun to develop your own style and technique, you may want to experiment with some of the more specialized equipment we mention.

Preparing the Design

Before you can cut a stencil, you'll have to transfer the design you've chosen, whether it's from this book or another source, to a piece of illustration board. In most cases, as you transfer the design you'll also resize it— a simple process we'll explain later. Here's a list of materials and tools used to transfer and enlarge designs.

Materials and Tools

Carbon paper or graphite paper: Carbon or graphite paper is used to transfer designs directly to illustration board when no resizing is necessary.

Illustration or poster board: Illustration board is a medium-weight cardboard with a smooth surface. It comes in two basic sizes: 15 by 20 inches and 20 by 30 inches. Always ask for single thickness. Although poster board, which is somewhat less expensive, will do the job, it's lighter in weight and therefore less durable.

Marking pens: It's best to draw your designs in pencil first and then trace over them with a black marking pen.

Pencils: Use a soft lead pencil (we prefer a 3B) when enlarging designs by the grid method, explained on page 14. The soft lead makes it easy to erase any mistakes.

Ruler: You'll use a ruler for both enlarging designs and cutting straight lines in stencils. A metal-edged one is best.

Spray adhesive, rubber cement, or white glue: In some cases, after tracing a design on tracing paper, it's necessary to adhere the paper to a piece of illustration board. Use spray adhesive, rubber cement, or white glue (Sobo or Elmer's, for instance) for this purpose. Follow manufacturers' directions.

Tracing paper: You'll use tracing paper when transferring designs that do not need to be resized. Tracing paper comes in many sizes, so make sure you buy paper large enough to cover your design.

Enlarging a Design

Each project in this book includes a stencil key: a design printed solid gray to use as a pattern from which to cut your stencils. Since it was impossible for us to print all our designs full size, it will be necessary to enlarge the stencil key before you actually cut your stencil. The easiest way to do this is simply to take the design to a photostating house (check your Yellow Pages) and have it enlarged to whatever size you wish. However, you'll find that the grid method is also surprisingly easy and accurate.

Over each of our stencil keys, we've printed a grid. No matter what the size of the printed key and grid, you'll always transfer it to a grid of one-inch squares. To begin, lightly number the boxes in pencil from top to bottom along one side and from left to right along the bottom.

Enlarging a Design

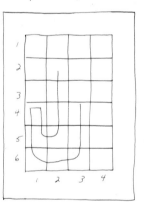

On a piece of illustration board, use a ruler to draw a grid of one-inch squares that has the same number of boxes as does the smaller, printed grid. Always leave a margin of at least two inches. Number the squares on the grid you've drawn in the same manner you numbered the printed grid.

Then, working square by square and using a soft lead pencil, duplicate the design in each square of the smaller grid in the corresponding square of the one-inch grid. After you've transferred the design, check to make sure you've drawn all the lines in the correct squares. Then trace over your pencil lines with a black marking pen, and you'll have a finished working key.

The grid method works for almost any design from any source. If, for example, you wanted to transfer a design from a magazine and you wanted to double its size, you could draw over it a grid of half-inch squares and then duplicate it on a grid of one-inch squares. By increasing the size of the squares in the grid you're transferring to, you can make your design as large as you wish.

Transferring a Design

To transfer any design that is actual size, simply place a sheet of tracing paper over the design and trace it in pencil. You can then glue the tracing paper to your illustration board, using spray adhesive (our preference), rubber cement, or white glue. You can also transfer your traced design to the board by placing a sheet of carbon or graphite paper face down on the board, placing the design on top of it, and tracing around the design. Then trace over the transferred design with black marking pen.

Creating Your Own Design

When you make designs from magazines, photographs, or other sources, you must be aware of stencil bridges. Bridges are the little sections of stencil left between the cutout shapes; they hold the stencil together and make it strong. They also, when carefully placed, enhance and become an integral part of the design. When using the stencil keys in this book to cut stencils, always cut out the gray shapes, leaving the white spaces between the gray shapes as bridges.

Let's say, for example, you want to make a stencil design from a photograph of a flower. Obviously, since you can't cut out one solid shape and expect it to look like the photo, you'll have to decide where to make bridges. It's best to make bridges that follow the contours of the object. Place a sheet of tracing paper over the photo and trace the lines with pencil; then expand each of the lines to ⅛ inch in width to create bridges. Mount the tracing paper on a piece of illustration board, and you're ready to use the design to cut a stencil.

Making Stencil Bridges

Start by making all your bridges about ⅛ inch wide. With experience, you'll learn that (1) sometimes a smaller bridge will do the job, (2) bridges should always be in proportion to the overall design, and that (3) the placement or elimination of some bridges can enhance a design.

In addition to stencils you cut yourself, a number of "found" objects can be used as stencils.

Doilies and lace: You can lay a doily or a piece of lace on any flat surface and then spray-paint over it. The prettier the doily or lace, the prettier the design.

Leaves and flowers: Leaves and flowers should always be pressed in a book for a week or so before using them as stencils. Then, you can either trace around them and make a regular stencil or place them directly on a flat surface, weight them with pebbles or coins, and spray-paint over them.

Templates: The templates used by artists and draftsmen to draw geometric shapes, such as circles and triangles, are perfect for stenciling. You can either trace through them with coloring tools or mask out the shapes you don't want and spray-paint through the remaining design. Available in art stores, templates are fairly expensive but last a lifetime.

Cutting the Stencil

Once you've made a working stencil key, you're ready to place stencil paper over it and cut your stencil. Although we almost always use commercially available stencil paper for our projects—and, on occasion, acetate—there are a number of materials from which stencils can be made.

Materials

Acetate: Because it's durable and washable, we use acetate for stencil designs that are to be repeated many times. Though virtually any design can be cut from acetate, for a first-time effort we recommend choosing a simple design with generally straight lines. Ask for .005-gauge. The least expensive way to buy acetate is in sheets that are 20 by 50 inches in size. It can also be purchased in tablets, usually of 25 sheets, in various sizes.

Architect's linen: Set designers and painters have used architect's linen for years. Stencils made from it hold up well, and intricate shapes can be cut into it with small manicure scissors.

Brown wrapping paper: Stencils can be made from brown wrapping paper by cutting the design and then coating each side of it with shellac.

Frisket paper: Traditionally used by those who stencil with airbrushes, the new frisket paper is a pressure-sensitive film of acetate. You can cut shapes from it, adhere the shapes to an object, paint over the shapes, and remove and discard the frisket.

Oiled stencil board and tagboard: Oiled stencil board is a cardboard that has been treated with oil to make it waterproof. Tagboard, so called because it's often used to make shipping tags, is similar to the cardboard from which manila folders are made. Tagboard is best for stencils that do not require paint because it is not waterproof. Because these boards are not transparent, the design must be transferred directly to them before cutting the stencil. For the same reason, neither can be used for modular stenciling. Although both boards are fairly widely used by stencilers, we find them a bit old-fashioned.

Soft woods: Thin sheets of soft wood can be used to make "relief" stencils. The stencil design is cut into the wood with saws, drills, knives, or chisels. The edges of the stencil design are beveled so that the bottom side is slightly larger than the top. Relief stenciling works best on bare plaster walls. Mix white glue with water—two parts water to one part white glue—and then add plaster to form a stiff putty. Hold the stencil firmly in place and force the putty through the stencil openings with a putty knife, trowel, or spatula; smooth the surface evenly and carefully remove the stencil. The beveled edges of the stencil will permit easy removal without damaging the design.

Stencil paper: As noted above, we prefer stencil paper for all projects that don't require a great deal of repetition—in which case we use acetate. Stencil paper is a white, waxed paper that's easy to cut and relatively durable. It's semitransparent, allowing you to place it over your stencil key and cut the stencil without retransferring the design. The transparency also allows you to do modular stenciling. Stencil paper, water-resistant and inexpensive, usually comes in a standard size of 18 by 24 inches. Ask for .005 thickness. It's readily available in art- and craft-supply stores.

Zinc or brass: In the past, thin sheets of zinc or brass have been used to make stencils that last virtually forever. If you wish, you too can make stencils from these materials, using files, awls, drills, or other sharp cutting tools to cut the design.

Tools

To cut stencils, we almost invariably use an X-acto knife, discussed in detail below. There are, however, other tools that can be used for cutting.

Paper punches: Paper punches can be used to punch holes in stencil paper and are especially helpful when cutting a design that has small, perfect circles or polka dots.

Razor blades: Single-edged razor blades can be used for cutting out large, relatively simple stencil shapes.

Scissors: As noted earlier, small manicure scissors are perfect for cutting stencils out of architect's linen.

Swivel knives: Used mainly for very complicated work, swivel knives are specially designed to cut curves. The ease with which they accomplish this purpose is somewhat offset by the fact that you must cut your design over a sheet of heavy glass to allow the blade to glide freely. And because the heavy glass would distort a stencil key placed under it, the stencil design must be transferred directly to the stencil paper before cutting with a swivel knife.

Utility knives: Also called mat knives and linoleum knives, these knives can be used in much the same way as razor blades—for cutting large, simple shapes.

X-acto knives: Although razor blades and utility knives will suffice in certain circumstances, we find the X-acto knife best as an all-around cutting tool—except for, of course, metal or wood stencils. We use the #1 X-acto knife handle with the #11 blade for virtually all stencil cutting, whether large or small, intricate or simple. This is what the knife and blade look like.

X-acto Knife

If you can't find the one we recommend, use one that has a similar shape. The blade of the knife should be changed often.

Miscellaneous Supplies

In addition to an X-acto knife and blade, and stencil paper or acetate— or whatever materials and tools you're using—there are several miscellaneous supplies that are helpful.

Masking tape: Masking tape is useful for taping stencil paper in place over the stencil key before cutting and for taping the finished stencil to the object to be decorated. Always test first to be sure the tape won't mar the surface. Masking tape can itself be used as a stencil: Affix the tape to an object, paint over it, and remove the tape.

Pushpins or thumbtacks: In some cases, thumbtacks or pushpins can be used as substitutes for masking tape.

Whetstones: Carborundum, oilstone, or other whetstones can be used to sharpen blades in a pinch. Generally speaking, however, since replacement blades are relatively inexpensive and simple to attach, it's easier simply to replace the blade.

Cutting Out the Design

After you have enlarged and transferred your stencil design to a sheet of illustration board, you're ready to cut your stencil. Measure the size of the design and then cut a piece of stencil paper—or whatever material you're working with—large enough to completely cover the design and still leave an ample margin, one to three inches, all around. A broad margin will not only make your stencil strong, it will also prevent unwanted spatters of color from getting on the object you're stenciling.

Using masking tape, tape the stencil paper over the working stencil key. Usually one small piece of tape on each side will be sufficient.

Although cutting a stencil is a simple process, it is very important always to have a sharp blade in your knife. This point cannot be stressed enough. Each cut in a stencil must be made in one, clean stroke. Going back over the lines more than once will result in an inferior stencil.

Always cut toward yourself with the knife perpendicular to the stencil paper, as shown in the illustration.

Cutting a Stencil

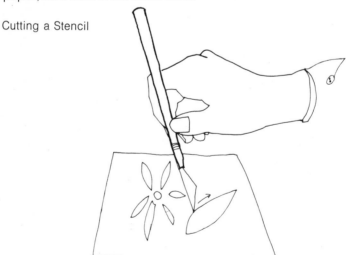

Hold the knife firmly and apply an even, steady pressure as you cut; experiment on scraps of stencil paper. You should be able to cut easily through the stencil paper without cutting too deeply into the illustration board. If you're cutting a large circle or a gentle curve, keep one hand free to turn the illustration board as you cut.

Because the stencil paper is strongest before you begin cutting out shapes, always start with small shapes and then move on to the larger ones. When cutting a design composed mainly of straight lines, cut horizontal lines first, then the vertical; use a metal-edged ruler to guide the blade. Practice at making perfect corners where your horizontal and vertical lines meet.

In some projects, you'll need to cut two stencils of the same design. either because you'll flop one stencil over to make a reverse design or because the design will be repeated so many times that one stencil would wear out before you finished. To cut two stencils simultaneously, tape one sheet of stencil paper over the working key and then tape a second over the first. Make sure you have a new blade in your knife and then, applying a little extra pressure, cut as you would for a single stencil.

You can occasionally stop and remove the cut sections to see how the work is progressing. When all the sections have been cut, carefully remove the tape and lift off the stencil. Stencils should be kept flat at all times. Do not roll them up, fold them, or stand them on edge.

Repairing a Stencil

Always exercise care when cutting around bridges. If you should happen to cut through or tear a bridge, place transparent tape on both sides of the stencil and then cut away the excess tape with your blade.

Repairing a Stencil

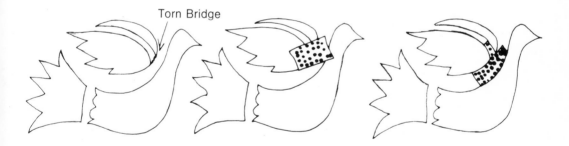

Torn Bridge

Stenciling the Object

There are lots of new materials on the market today that make stenciling easier and more fun. Acrylic and latex paints dry quickly and are water-soluble when wet but waterproof when dry. Marking pens are also relatively new on the art scene, and they also come in hundreds of colors.

Color Applicators

In most of our projects, we've used stencil brushes, marking pens, spray paint, or pieces of sponge to apply color; there are, however, many other applicators that can be used to achieve different effects.

Airbrushes: The airbrush is a very special color applicator used mainly by professional artists. Used to apply thin mists of color, the apparatus consists of an air compressor attached by hose to an adjustable tip. Paint or ink is placed in a special container that attaches to the brush; air is forced through the hose, which in turn sprays paint from the airbrush. Compressors range in price from about $50 to about $300, and airbrushes range from about $20 to $100.

Badger blender: Found mainly in sign-makers' shops but also in some art and stationery stores, the badger blender is a special stenciling brush made with extremely soft bristles to make it possible to create subtle shading effects.

Glue brushes: Glue brushes are similar to stencil brushes (see below) but are softer. They are usually very large and therefore best for large designs, such as floors and walls.

Marking pens: Marking pens are especially good for stenciling on light-colored paper or cardboard. They also can be used on unfinished wood. Although they come with both permanent and nonpermanent inks, we recommend the nonpermanent because they bleed less—through capillary action—than do the permanent ones. If you use a pen with permanent ink, you'll have to work very quickly to prevent your finished design from appearing fuzzy. After stenciling a paper item with nonpermanent markers, which are available in a wide variety of colors, you may want to protect the design with a spray fixative or protective coating. When using a marking pen, hold it perpendicular to the paper and make clean, even strokes. If you trace back over your lines, the paper will show wear and tear and the final design will appear scruffy. Marking pens are not suitable for all stencils; those with long, thin bridges will not be strong enough to support the pressure from the pen.

Paint rollers: Paint rollers can be used to apply paint through the openings of fairly large stencils. Dip the roller in a small amount of paint and then roll off the excess on newspaper; excess paint will run under the edges of the stencil and ruin the design. It's best to apply two light coats rather than one heavy one.

Watercolor brushes: Small watercolor brushes with pointed tips are good for stenciling on food with food coloring. They can also be used for touching up most projects.

Sponges: Sponges are perfect for stenciling with colored inks, watercolors, and watered-down acrylic paints. Make sure to wring out the sponge until it's fairly dry; otherwise, color will run under the stencil and spoil the design. Sponges are also useful for creating subtle shading effects. For either purpose, buy a household sponge and cut it into one-inch-wide strips, cutting across the width of the sponge. Use one strip for each color you're stenciling, and dip only the tip of the strip into the color. The texture of the sponge will show in the final design.

Stencil brushes: The classic stenciling applicators, stencil brushes always have a blunt end; the best ones are made of hogs' hair. They come in a variety of sizes that get larger along with their number. Since different manufacturers use different numbering systems, here's an actual-size illustration of what we mean when we call for a given brush size.

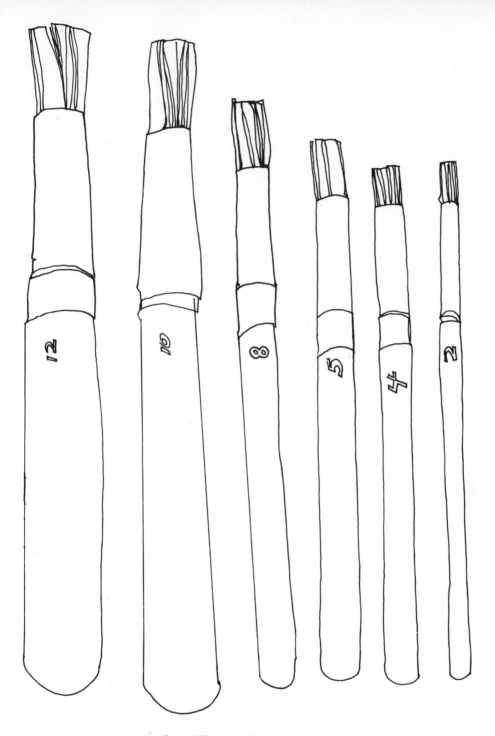

Stencil Brushes (Actual Size)

Since stencil brushes are inexpensive and because you should always start with a clean, dry brush, it's a good idea to have plenty of brushes on hand. However, if you want to change colors and you run short of brushes, you can clean a brush and speed the drying process with a hair blower. There is a special stenciling brush, often used by sign makers, called a poonah; it has a relatively soft bristle and a long handle and is ideal for many projects in this book. The bristles of stencil brushes come in various degrees of stiffness; with experimentation, you'll find the one that suits you best. We prefer softer bristles; stiff bristles not only wear out stencils quickly, they tend to "bounce" off the object you're stenciling.

Toothbrushes: To achieve a speckled texture, use a toothbrush to spatter paint through stencil openings. Be sure to mask out areas where you don't want paint.

Velour: Wrapping velour around your index finger, dipping it in paint, and then stenciling with an up-and-down dabbing motion or a soft rubbing motion will give a subtle effect. Velvets and other soft fabrics also work well.

Coloring Media

In most of our projects, we've used either acrylic paints or marking pens. In certain cases, we've called for ink, japan colors, spray paint, or food coloring. There are, however, many different media that can be used in stenciling. Again, we've tried to be as comprehensive as possible; don't be overwhelmed by the great variety of possibilities.

Acrylic paints: We highly recommend acrylic paints as an all-around stenciling medium. You can stencil with these paints directly from the tubes; their consistency is perfect for making crisp designs. They come in dozens of colors, dry quickly, and all brands are compatible with one another. Acrylics are very durable and adhere best to washable fabrics, wood, surfaces painted with flat latex or flat latex enamel, paper, cardboard, unglazed ceramics, many plastics (test for permanence), straw and woven items, metal (galvanized or nonslick), and leather. Fabrics stenciled with acrylic paints can be washed in warm water with soap after the paint has dried for at least forty-eight hours; do not dry-clean.

Batik dyes and dye thickener: You can add dye thickener to batik dye until the mixture is thick enough to allow you to stencil your design onto fabric with a stencil brush. Both are available at specialty dye shops as well as some craft-supply stores. The charm of using dyes is in the transparency of the stenciled design.

Ceramic supplies: Such ceramic supplies as engobes, underglazes, overglazes, and stains can be used to stencil on ceramics using a fine brush or an airbrush. You can also create an intaglio effect in ceramics by carving through stencil openings into leather-hard clay.

Crayons, pens, and pencils: Almost any writing implement can be used for stenciling on paper or cardboard. Crayons, pens, and pencils are also good for planning and testing designs.

Food coloring: We use food coloring to stencil pie crusts, cookies, and breads. It is usually mixed with egg yolk and then painted onto raw dough with a small brush; breads, however, are stenciled after baking. We've also successfully used small bits of sponge to apply food coloring. It should be noted that certain types of food coloring are considered to be unhealthful; investigate before buying.

Japan colors: Designed to adhere to slick surfaces, japan colors dry very quickly. Use them on glass, enameled, or shiny metal surfaces, such as autos, refrigerators, or glazed ceramic items. Since japan colors are very thin, you should always work with a fairly dry brush; use one or two thin coats rather than one heavy one when needed. Use turpentine or paint thinner to clean brushes.

Latex paints: Both flat and enamel latex paints are exceptionally good for stenciling. With them, you can match the color of the design you're stenciling to the color of your room. They are water-soluble when wet, allowing easy cleanup, but permanent when dry. Like japan colors, latex paints dry quickly and are thin in consistency; stencil with a fairly dry brush. Use soap and water to clean brushes. Latex paints can be used in any project that calls for acrylic paints.

Oil paints: Oil paints can be used on slick surfaces or any surface that you might use acrylic paint on. They do, however, take a long time to dry; use them only for full-image stencils. Clean brushes with turpentine or paint thinner.

Patio and deck paints: If you use patio or deck paint on a floor or patio, you'll need no further protection, such as varnish. However, since these paints dry very slowly, you'll need to plan your design carefully. Avoid designs that require overlapping stencils unless you allow adequate drying time; choose a randomly scattered design, or cut a large stencil that has several repeated designs in it. The consistency of these paints is thin; stencil with a fairly dry brush. Clean brushes with turpentine or paint thinner.

Poster paints: Use poster paints to stencil on paper or cardboard for effective signs or school projects. Work with a fairly dry brush. Since poster paints are nonpermanent, you can clean up with soap and water.

Sizing: Sizing for gold leaf can be stenciled, allowed to dry until agressively tacky, and gold or silver leaf applied.

Spray paints: When using aerosol-spray paints, be sure to leave a wide margin around the cutouts in your stencil to prevent paint from getting where it shouldn't be. It's sometimes helpful when spray-painting to weight down the stencil with small stones or other objects to prevent paint from seeping under the edges of the stencils. You can also adhere a stencil to an object with nonpermanent spray adhesive or rubber cement; the adhesive can be removed when the spray paint is dry. As with most paints, one or two light coats are preferable to one heavy one.

Textile paints: Designed especially for fabrics, textile paints are usually thick enough to achieve nice, crisp stenciled designs. Follow directions of the manufacturer.

Watercolors, colored inks, and india ink: Colored inks and watercolors are transparent; india ink is a dense black. All are good for stenciling on paper, especially watercolor paper. We prefer to use sponge strips with these media, but a fine sable brush will also work.

Wax: You can stencil with wax and a tjanting needle onto cotton or silk fabrics and then dye the fabric with cold-water batik dyes for a special batik effect. A tjanting needle is an instrument that is held and used like a pen and that is fitted out with a reservoir on top for hot wax.

Stenciling with Paints

In general, whenever stenciling with paint, you should first dip the tip of the brush into the paint and then remove all excess by "pouncing" the brush up and down on newspaper. To prevent paint from running under the edges of the stencil openings, you should always work with a fairly dry brush. The thinner the paint, the more care that must be taken. When working with thin paint, pounce the brush several extra times.

Always hold the stencil brush perpendicular to the stencil you're working on. An up-and-down dabbing motion should always be used to apply paint with a stencil brush; do not stroke. In some cases, it may be necessary to apply more than one coat of paint to achieve the desired brilliancy or evenness of tone.

Using a Stencil Brush

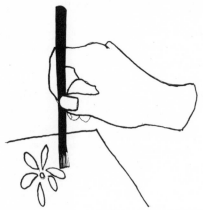

To ensure crisp designs, it is of prime importance that the stencil remain stationary and as close as possible to the surface being stenciled. Usually, the stencil will be held in place by masking tape, tacks, pins, or paper clips. As you stencil, use your free hand to press down the edges of the stencil opening closest to the area where you're applying color.

Stenciling around Bridges

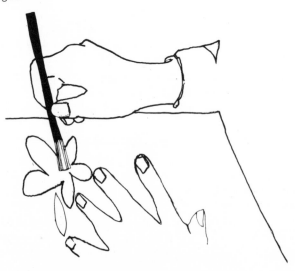

When stenciling a design that has bridges that are either very small or long and narrow, use a pencil, pen, or other pointed instrument to hold down each bridge as you stencil around it.

Stenciling around
Bridges

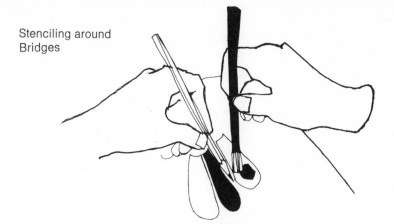

Since it is the cleanness of the outside line of a design that determines whether the design will be crisp or fuzzy, take special care with this area. Do the outside edges first, making sure that your brush is fairly dry and holding the edges of the stencil down firmly. Once the outside line has been filled in crisply, you can apply a little extra paint to the center area.

Before you stencil an actual object, it's always best to do a bit of experimenting. First, stencil the design on paper with marking pens, cut it out, and fit it onto the object you plan to stencil. This process will give you an idea of how best to situate the design. It's also a good idea to practice stenciling the design with paint—or whatever medium you plan to use—on a scrap of wood or cardboard to gain an understanding of the characteristics of the paint you're using.

Don't be dismayed if your designs aren't absolutely perfect; slightly inconsistent or imperfect designs are part of the charm of stenciling. Remember, stenciling is a handcraft and is not intended to be machinelike in perfection.

Shading and Highlighting

Shaded
Rectangle

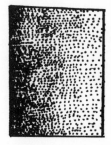

Shading and highlighting can add both interest and a three-dimensional quality to a stenciled design. There are four basic ways to create shading/highlighting.

Let's assume you want to stencil a shaded rectangle. Dip the tip of the stencil brush into a small amount of paint and pounce the brush on newspaper. Begin stenciling on the left side and work toward the right. As you begin, there will be a high concentration of paint; as you move toward the right, using up paint, the value will become lighter. Practice doing this until the transition from dark to light is a smooth one.

You can also apply a thin (pounce the brush several extra times) coat of paint and then apply a second coat of paint in those areas you want to be more intense.

A third shading technique is to stencil the entire shape with one color first and, leaving the stencil in place, allow it to dry. Then stencil part of the shape with a second color, taking care to blend the colors smoothly. You could, for instance, stencil a leaf shape in medium green and then shade the leaf in certain areas with dark blue.

Light-colored highlights can add a spark to dark-toned designs. Let's say you've stenciled a shape in medium blue. Leave the stencil in place and allow the paint to dry. Then mix a small amount of white paint into the medium blue and apply highlights in chosen areas, stenciling over the first coat of paint.

Mixing and Matching Colors

Mixing colors is a craft in itself, and because there are numerous books and discussions of the subject, we won't go into it in great detail. Besides, with the hundreds of different colors of acrylic paints, latex paints, inks, markers, and spray paints available today, it's seldom necessary to mix your own colors.

One line of acrylic paints, made by Liquitex, is called Modular Colors. Each color in this line is graded on a value scale. For instance, if you were buying a tube of red paint, you could choose any red ranging from a very pale one (Value 9) to a very dark one (Value 3) to one that is very dark and deep (Base Value). There are also several other brands of acrylic paints that will give professional results: Grumbacher Hyplar, Bocour Aqua-Tec, and Shiva.

Latex paints also come in a very wide range of premixed and custom-mixed colors; with them it is possible to match almost any color scheme.

If you wish to mix your own colors, we suggest you first obtain a color wheel (most encyclopedias include a color wheel under the heading "color"). It takes experience to mix colors well, and the best way to learn is by experimenting. Keep on hand several medium-sized bristle brushes just for mixing. You may also want to try mixing paints with a palette knife, though we find a #8 bristle brush is best for mixing acrylic paints. We keep lots of small pieces of cardboard around to squeeze out and scrape off excess paint from the mixing brush. When we mix colors, we do so on paper plates made from recycled paper; they're disposable and inexpensive. You can also save small plastic containers that various foods come in; if they have tight-fitting lids, your paint will remain usable for a long time.

Mitering Corners

The easiest way to turn a corner when stenciling a border design is to miter the edges of the two design elements where they meet. To do this, center the end of a strip of masking tape at the corner of the surface being stenciled and lay down enough tape so that it will intersect the border. (The tape should form a 45-degree angle with the edges of the surface you're stenciling.) When you come to the tape, continue stenciling the design onto it, as shown in Figure A of the illustration. Then remove the tape and allow the design to dry. Reposition the tape so that its outer edge corresponds exactly to the edge of the design just stenciled. Stencil the intersecting border, again continuing the design onto the tape, as shown in Figure B of the illustration. When the tape is removed, you should have a professionally mitered corner, as shown in Figure C of the illustration.

Mitering
Corners

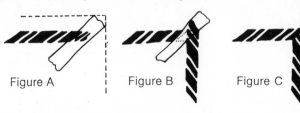

Figure A   Figure B   Figure C

Protecting the Design

Sometimes your stenciled designs will require a protective coating. There are many such coatings: polyurethane, varnishes, spray fixatives, and shellacs. In each of our projects, we'll tell you what type of protection, if any, is required for a particular surface. Always test protective coatings to make sure they are clear enough; use the bottom of the object you're stenciling or a scrap of a similar surface.

Miscellaneous Stenciling Supplies

In addition to the tools and materials we've already discussed in detail, there are a number of other items that are helpful in stenciling.

Chalk or tailor's chalk can be used to make guidelines or registration marks. We prefer tailor's chalk in pencil form; it's easy to handle and is easily removed when finished.

Detergent is used, along with warm water, to wash brushes after they have been cleaned with the proper solvent. Ideally, brushes should be hung to dry with the bristles pointing down, but it's also acceptable to let them dry in a horizontal position. When wet, brushes should never be placed in a position with the bristles pointing upward; moisture will seep into the metal ferrule surrounding the bristles and eventually destroy the brush.

Nonpermanent spray adhesive is the only spray glue we recommend. Check to make sure that it's removable with rubber cement thinner (see below) before using.

Paint thinner or turpentine is used to clean brushes, hands, and supplies after using japan colors, oil paints, oil-based enamel paints, deck paint, or any other paint that calls for turpentine as a thinner.

Paper plates are used to mix paints on or as a palette to hold paint while stenciling.

Paper towels are great for cleanup work.

Plastic spoons are good for mixing small cans of paints, such as japan color; also use them to scoop paint from can to paper plate.

Rubber cement is good for attaching stencils to hard surfaces, such as wood, metal, and enamel. Apply a thin coat to the surface and a thin coat to the wrong side of the stencil. Allow the cement to dry; then *carefully* attach the stencil (the stencil will instantly stick to the surface and you won't be able to reposition it without regluing). Use an eraser to remove rubber cement from the stencil openings, taking care not to damage the stencil. You can also use rubber cement to make a "disappearing" stencil: Use rubber cement to brush a design directly onto an object, paint over the design with spray paint or acrylic paint. Paint will not adhere to the area covered with rubber cement. When the paint has dried, remove the rubber cement with an eraser or with rubber cement thinner.

Rubber cement thinner is used to remove rubber cement from a stenciled object after the paint has thoroughly dried. It is also used to remove Spra-Mount, a trade name for a nonpermanent spray adhesive. Rubber cement thinner will not damage acrylic, enamel, or latex finishes.

Fabrics should be clean, dry, and wrinkle-free; if necessary, press fabric with an iron or have a dry cleaner press it. It's usually a good idea to stretch fabric taut and pin it to a board before stenciling. When stenciling a garment, place a layer of newspaper or a piece of cardboard inside to keep color from bleeding through to the back. Test paints or dyes on fabric scraps before beginning; some paints will look unattractive on dark fabrics unless you stencil the design white and let it dry before stenciling the desired color. *Acrylic paints* are good for washable fabrics, such as cotton, silk, and polyester. As you stencil, use the stencil brush to force the paint into the weave of the fabric. If you find this difficult, thin the paint with a drop of water. Generally speaking, the heavier the fabric, the thinner the paint can be. *Textile paints* should be used on fabrics that must be dry-cleaned; they may also be used on washables. As with acrylics, the color should be forced into the weave of the fabric with the stencil brush. Do not thin textile paints unless working with very absorbent fabric. Textile paints vary greatly; be sure to follow manufacturer's instructions. *Cold-water (batik) dyes* and *dye thickeners* can be used on washable fabrics. Add enough thickener to the dye to bring it to the proper consistency for stenciling. Again, use the stencil brush to force color into the weave of the fabric. Dyes are transparent; choose white or light-colored fabrics and "build up" colors. Remember that the color of the fabric will affect the dye; blue dye on yellow fabric, for instance, will result in a green color. Be sure to follow manufacturer's directions for "setting" the dye and removing the thickener. Because of the transparency of dyes, their effect is very different from that of opaque paint. *Other fabric ideas:* Stencil your design in pencil on an iron-on patch, cut it out, and iron into place; stencil your design with pencil, acrylics, or a needlepoint marker and then embroider it; stencil with a hot wax your design and then batik it.

Pick-of-the-Crop
Cookout Coverall

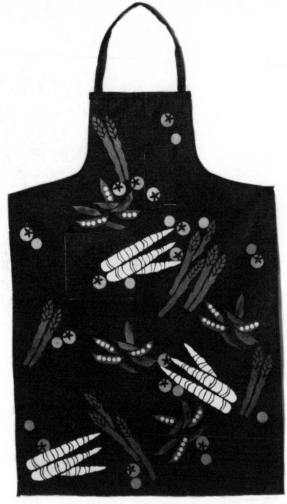

George, a 250-pound ex-marine, has a heavy-duty exterior that belies his gentle nature. Besides a number of other positive attributes, George can cook. For one whole summer we gorged ourselves on his sumptuous meals, spending hours around the old wooden table in his garden.

The only thing George had yet to master was the art of French cuisine. Late that summer, he heard about a Frenchwoman who had rented a restaurant kitchen and was conducting cooking classes. George enrolled. It was an intensive course (four nights a week), and we weren't able to see much of George. We decided to pay him a surprise visit, hoping along the way to sample his newly acquired skills.

We were escorted to the kitchen. When he turned around and saw the lot of us, George promptly turned a glowing shade of crimson. Why the colorful greeting? Our friend, big, bulky George, was turned out in a frilly, fluffy, pink apron. Let it be understood that George does not have a fetish for pink aprons. It was simply that the dictatorial Madame Farnaud required all her students, male or female, to be properly attired.

The next day we bought an industrial blue apron and stenciled an assortment of fresh vegetables on it. The apron, greatly appreciated, has become old and worn, but it was so well loved that we've done another and included it here.

Materials:

man's blue denim work apron
1 piece illustration board, 20 by 30 inches
masking tape
1 sheet stencil paper, 18 by 24 inches
#1 X-acto knife with #11 blades
newspaper
acrylic tube paints, in green, orange, white, and red
paper plates
7 stencil brushes, all #5

Procedure:

1.   Enlarge all the stencil designs to size on the illustration board (see page 14), leaving at least 2 inches of space between designs. Tape the sheet of stencil paper over the designs. Then, using the X-acto knife, cut the stencils one at a time. Since circles are more difficult to cut than straight lines or gentle curves, you may want to practice first. When cutting circles, turn the board with one hand while you cut with the other. As you finish cutting each stencil, cut around it, allowing at least a 1-inch border all around.

2.   Spread a layer of newspaper over a work surface large enough to enable you to lay the apron out flat. Spread out the apron, right side up. You will first be using the two asparagus stencils. Since you will be using these stencils several times, look carefully at the illustration to see where the stencils should be placed.

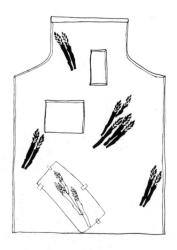

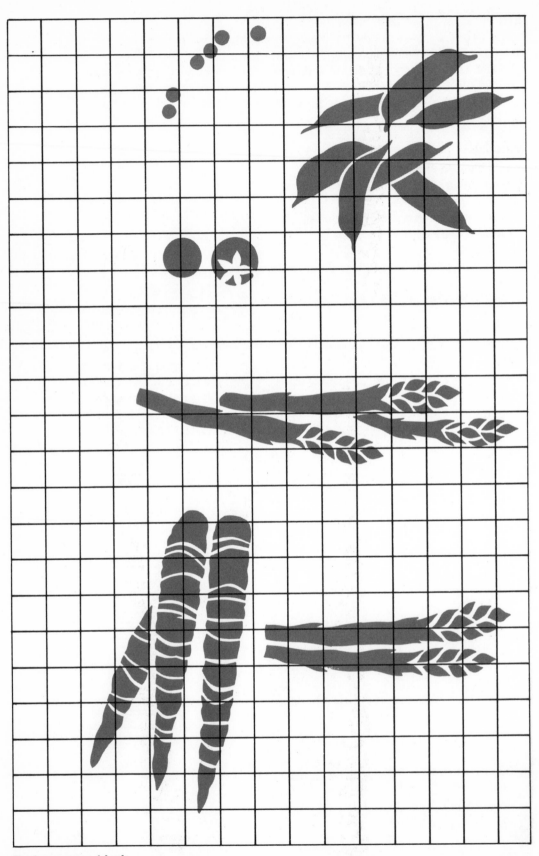

Each square = 1 inch

Then tape one of the stencils in place on the apron to make the first asparagus design. Squeeze a small amount of green paint onto a paper plate, dip the tip of a stencil brush into the paint, and remove the excess by pouncing the brush on newspaper until the brush is fairly dry. Begin stenciling by gently dabbing the brush through the openings with an up-and-down motion. Continue adding color until all the openings have been filled. Because you are stenciling a light color on a darker background, you'll need to apply two coats of paint: Leave the stencil taped in place until the first coat is dry to the touch; then apply the second coat. Carefully lift up the stencil and position it for the next asparagus design. Repeat the process—tape, stencil, let dry, apply second coat, and reposition—until your apron shows as many asparagus designs as does the illustration.

3.   In this step, you'll stencil carrots onto the apron. The illustration shows where they should be placed.

Using orange paint on a clean paper plate and a clean, dry brush, stencil the carrots as you did the asparagus.

4.   To add the pea pods to the apron, check the illustration for the proper placements, tape the stencil in place for the first repeat, and stencil it as you did the asparagus and carrots, using green paint on a clean paper plate and a clean, dry brush. Add all the pea pods in the same manner.

5.   Next place the peas—the small circular stencils—directly over the pea-pod designs, making sure that the circles are within the pod shapes; then tape them in place.

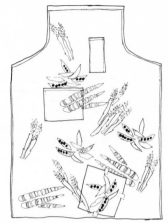

Using a lighter green paint obtained by mixing some white in with the green, stencil the peas. They require only one coat of paint.

6.   The final step is the application of the tomatoes. After checking the illustration for placements, tape the two tomato stencils in place.

Since red is a very transparent color, you will first need to stencil the tomatoes white, using a clean paper plate for the paint and a clean, dry brush. When the white paint is completely dry, squeeze some red paint onto a clean paper plate and apply it over the white with a clean stencil brush. Do not remove the stencil between coats. Stencil as many tomatoes in this way as are shown in the illustration, alternating the stencils as necessary.

7.   The apron is now finished. Clean your brushes with water and paper towels. The paint on the apron will seem a bit stiff when it is dry; to remedy this, let the apron dry for 48 hours and then wash it in warm water with normal laundry detergent. Do not dry-clean it.

Hints and Ideas:

★ To stencil more quickly, cut more than one stencil of each design.

Dressed-Up Sling Back

In resistance to the rising cost of furniture, people these days are inventive in their approaches to decorating a house or apartment. One solution is to take inexpensive patio or deck furniture and bring it indoors, making it work by either accessorizing the room to match or by somehow changing the original piece of furniture.

We've taken a modestly priced canvas sling-backed chair and stenciled it with a bold supergraphic design of intricately woven cords. It's an easy project that adds a whole new dimension to a nicely designed but otherwise ordinary chair. Not only will this expensive-looking design dress up fabric, it will look exciting on a wall, a floor, or even a refrigerator.

Materials:
canvas sling-backed chair, in a natural color and with removable canvas
1 piece illustration board, 15 by 20 inches
scissors
1 sheet stencil paper, 18 by 24 inches
masking tape
#1 X-acto knife with #11 blades
newspaper
iron (optional)
yardstick
tailor's chalk, in a pastel color
acrylic tube paint, in brown
paper plate
1 stencil brush, #10

Procedure:

1. Enlarge the stencil design to size on the illustration board (see page 14). Trim the stencil paper slightly smaller than the illustration board and tape it in place over the design. Using the X-acto knife, cut out the design and then cut around it, leaving at least a 1-inch border.

2. Cover a work surface with newspaper. Then remove the canvas from the chair and lay it out flat on the newspaper. Make sure that it is flat and wrinkle-free. If necessary, press it with a hot iron. Then, using a yardstick, find the center of the width of the canvas. Draw a guideline all the way down the center with the tailor's chalk. Then draw two more guidelines, each 6½ inches from the center guideline and running parallel to it, as shown.

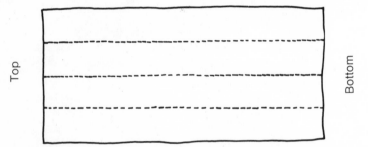

3. Place the stencil at the top of the canvas, using the chalk guidelines to center it correctly, as shown.

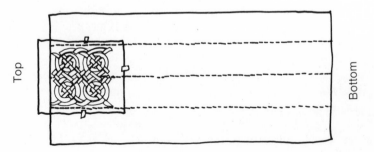

Tape the stencil into place. Squeeze a small amount of brown paint onto a paper plate, dip the tip of the brush into the paint, and remove the excess by pouncing it on some newspaper. Using an up-and-down dabbing motion, apply the paint through the openings until all the openings have been coated. Remove the stencil and let the paint dry to the touch.

4.   Reposition the stencil below the section you have just completed. The openings at the top of the stencil should almost meet the bottom of the design previously stenciled, with about ¼ inch of space separating them. Use the chalk guidelines to center it. Following the stenciling procedure described in step 3, stencil the design. Continue to repeat the design until it runs the length of the canvas. (On our chair, it was necessary to repeat it 2½ more times, meaning that the last half ran off the canvas onto the newspaper.)

5.   When you have completed the stenciling, clean the brush with water. When the design is completely dry—about 2 hours—remove the tailor's chalk by rubbing over it with a damp sponge. Then replace the canvas on the frame of the chair.

Hints and Ideas:

★Stencil this design on a fabric shower curtain with acrylic paints.

Tropical Towel

After a long (seven years) and stormy courtship, David once again asked Laura for her hand in marriage, and once again Laura said yes. To our surprise, however, she also added, "And this time I really mean it!" Having been close friends with the two during those seven years, we all breathed a sigh of relief and hoped that June would signal the beginning of a marriage that would somehow be less erratic than their engagement had been.

Laura was more than radiant, and though we saw less of her, we knew her intense happiness was marred by one minor problem: She wanted the world to share the fact that she finally, unconditionally, and irrevocably loved David. After considering hiring sky writers (too expensive) and printing lots of little slips of paper with "All will go well now that Laura loves David" and slipping them into fortune cookies (too time-consuming), we hit on a perfect solution.

Since they were planning to honeymoon on a tropical isle, why not stencil Laura's sentiment on a beach towel and sprinkle it with a few lush palms? Fellow sun worshippers would, at least, get the message.

Stenciling is the easiest way to personalize almost any item with stunning, professional results. In Laura's case, we not only stenciled her message, we also perked up the towel with a design appropriate to locale. You could, for example, stencil your initials on a set of towels and add a design that appears in the design of your bathroom wallpaper. We've included a complete alphabet for this project so that you can stencil any message you wish. We hope it's as joyous as Laura's.

Materials:

large beach towel, in yellow
1 piece illustration board, 15 by 20 inches
scissors
1 sheet stencil paper, 18 by 24 inches
masking tape
#1 X-acto knife with #11 blades
newspaper
acrylic tube paints, in bright red and dark green
paper plates
2 stencil brushes, one #4 and one #5
marking pen

Procedure:

1. Transfer each of the stencil designs below to the illustration board (see page 15), leaving at least 2 inches between the designs. Decide on a message that you want to stencil and enlarge the necessary letters, found

Palm-Trunk Section Stencil

Palm Frond Stencil

Half-Leaf Stencil

on page 117, on the same illustration board. Be sure to leave about 2 inches between the letters. Cut the stencil paper into three sections and tape one sheet over the palm-trunk section and the letters. Cut out the designs, using the X-acto knife. Then cut around each design, leaving at least a 1-inch border all around. Tape the other two stencil-paper sections—one on top of the other—over the palm frond and the half-leaf. Using a fresh blade in the X-acto knife, cut out both designs. Finally, cut around them, leaving at least a 1-inch margin all around. You should have two each of these two stencils.

2.   Cover the top of a large work surface with newspaper and spread the towel out flat on top. Since you will be stenciling the message first, let the right-hand edge of the towel hang down over the edge of the work surface if necessary. Then squeeze a small amount of red paint onto a paper plate and dip the tip of the #5 brush into the paint. Pounce the brush on some newspaper to remove the excess paint. Position the first letter stencil on the towel and hold it firmly in place with your fingers.

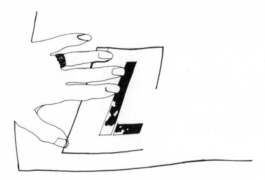

Dab the paint through the openings of the stencil, using an up-and-down motion. When you have stenciled the first letter, carefully lift up the stencil and go on to the next letter. Continue this process until you have stenciled all the letters in your message. When you have completed a word, leave a wide space (about 5 inches) before you begin the next word. You can arrange your message in a straight line, as shown in the illustration, or in a sweeping curve, as shown in the project photograph.

3.   The stencil for the palm trunk is a modular one, which means that it is a section to be repeated over and over to make a complete design. The illustration shows how it is done.

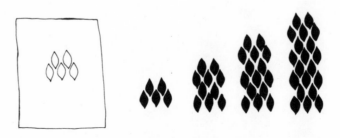

Squeeze a small amount of green paint onto a clean paper plate, dip the tip of the #4 brush into the paint, and pounce the bristles on some newspaper to remove the excess. Position the stencil at the lower left-hand corner of the towel, tape it firmly in place, and stencil the bottom of one palm trunk. Working toward the right, stencil the bases of all the palm trees, placing a base in each space between words and one in the lower right-hand corner of the towel.

Then return to the left-hand side of the towel and stencil in the next portion of each tree. Continue this "building" process, staggering the heights of the palms to achieve a natural effect, until all the trunks are finished.

4.   Now add the fronds to the tops of the trunks. Separate the two palm-leaf stencils that you have cut, turn one of them over, and place both in front of you so that they point in different directions. Using small strips of masking tape and a marking pen, label the one pointing to the left A-1 and the other A-2.

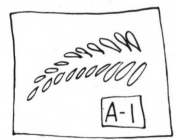

5.   Tape stencil A-1 on the left side of the top of the first palm trunk. Still using the green paint and following the same stenciling procedure described in step 3, stencil the fronds. Repeat the fronds on all the trees until the towel looks like this.

6.　Tape stencil A-2 on the right side of the top of the first palm trunk and stencil it. Add the stencil A-2 design to the right side of all the trees.

7.　Continue alternating stencil A-1 with stencil A-2 until the tops of all the palms are thick with foliage. After your trees look similar to this,

randomly stencil the half-leaf design among the leaves you have already stenciled, as shown in the illustration.

Adding these to the trees makes them look a bit more delicate.

8.　Your towel is now finished. Clean your brushes with water and paper towels, and let the paint dry thoroughly before you take it to the beach. Wait 48 hours before laundering the towel.

Hints and Ideas:
★Since the palm-trunk stencil is modular, you could stencil a wall with a ceiling-high palm tree.

Olive-Branch Summer Dress

As long as there have been dressmakers, there have been textile designers. Though the cut of a dress is definitely an important part of fashion, it's often the fabric design that moves the eye and spirit.

This project shows you how you can decorate and create your own designs on fabric. A simple, long white T-shirt dress in this case—a cool summer classic. The print on the dress was designed for a friend who vacationed in Greece. Hence, the olive branch, symbol of peace and prosperity.

To keep this project simple, the stencils are based on a modular concept. This means that you cut relatively small stencils and use them over and over. If you had to cut one complete stencil for the entire dress, it would mean cutting 24 branches, 208 leaves, and 127 olives. So we've done it the easy way. We cut only four stencils and then repeated them until the pattern wound its way from the top of the dress down and around the body to the bottom of the dress.

The effect? A devastatingly elegant pattern that completely transformed a basic, inexpensive dress. A dress as cool and fresh as the Aegean breeze that rustles the trees in the early hours of the morning.

Materials:
1 ankle-length cotton-knit dress*
1 piece illustration board, 20 by 30 inches
masking tape
2 sheets stencil paper, each 18 by 24 inches
#1 X-acto knife with #11 blades
marking pen
newspaper
1 piece cardboard, 18 by 24 inches
acrylic tube paints, in dark green, dark olive, light olive, and dark,
**   dusty purple**
paper plates
4 stencil brushes, all #4

*Since dry-cleaning fluids tend to fade or remove acrylic paints from fabric, be sure to choose a dress that is washable.

Procedure:
1.   Before you begin stenciling, notice that, in general, the finished design of the dress consists of two gentle spirals of olive branches. One spiral starts on the front at the neckline and winds its way down across the side seam and onto the back; the other starts high on the back and flows down and across to the other side seam and onto the front.

Front   Back

To do this, we began at the neckline of the front of the dress and randomly stenciled the two olive-branch designs in a general spiral configuration. Since we wanted the final effect to be delicate and feminine, we took care not to overload the dress with branches.

2. Enlarge all four stencil designs to size on the illustration board (see page 14), leaving at least 2 inches of space between them. Tape two sheets of stencil paper over the designs. Using a new blade in your X-acto knife, cut out the designs and then cut around them, leaving at least a 1-inch margin all around. Separate each set of designs and turn one of each set over. As you stencil, use some the way you cut them and use some in reverse, to add variety to the design.

3. Before you begin stenciling, cover a large work surface with newspaper. Lay the dress, front side up, out flat on top, and slide the piece of cardboard inside the dress, trimming the cardboard to fit if necessary.

Tape the large olive-branch stencil to the left side of the dress at the neckline and adjust the cardboard so that it is directly under it. The cardboard will prevent the other side of the dress from absorbing unwanted paint.

4. Squeeze a bit of dark green paint onto one paper plate and some of the dark olive onto another. Dip the tip of a brush into each color, pounce the bristles of each brush on some newspaper to remove the excess paint, and begin stenciling by dabbing the color through the branch and leaf openings. Do some dark green and some dark olive. Move the board down so that it's below the area just stenciled and add more branches and leaves in the same manner, alternating colors and branch stencils. Shift the board down again and under the side seam, and continue to add branches and leaves. To complete the first spiral, shift the board to the lower edge of the back of the dress and add more branches and leaves.

5. When the paint on the front of the dress is dry, turn the dress over and stencil the design on the back. Start at the left side of the neckline and follow exactly the same stenciling procedure described in steps 2 and 3. When you've completed the second spiral, clean your brushes and let them dry.

6. Squeeze small amounts of light olive and dark purple paint on separate paper plates. Using clean, dry brushes and holding one of the olive stencils in place with your fingers, stencil olives throughout the branches, alternating colors and olive stencils as you wish. Concentrate the olives in some areas and stencil them sparsely in others. Clean your brushes and allow the paint to dry for one hour before you wear the dress.

Hints and Ideas:

★Although you can wear the dress after the paint has dried, don't wash it for 48 hours. This dress—because it's made of a natural fiber—can safely be machine-laundered on a delicate wash cycle. You can also handwash it in a cold-water soap. Do not dry-clean it.

★Try creating your own design with these stencils—a border around a hem or a design that's shaped like an actual olive tree, for instance.

★This same set of stencils can be used to stencil a matching scarf or shawl.

Monogrammed Tote

Status accessories—handbags, luggage, and other items that have been imprinted with the initials of "in" designers—sometimes soar to amazing heights of absurdity. Not long ago there appeared on the market a miniscule shoulder bag that retailed for about $500. Now, we know that quality is expensive, but nobody has ever explained, at least to our satisfaction, exactly what it is that a $500 bag does that a $50 bag doesn't do.

At any rate, we thought perhaps you'd like to create your own status bag with your own initials—or anyone else's, for that matter. All you have to do is cut a few small designs and a pair of initials and repeat them until you've covered the surface of the tote. Just think of all the money you'll save to buy things that really matter: sable coats, private jets, rare jewels....

Materials:

canvas tote bag, *in a natural color or white
1 piece illustration board, 15 by 20 inches
masking tape
1 sheet stencil paper, 18 by 24 inches
#1 X-acto knife with #11 blades
books, magazines, *or* **newspapers, for stuffing the bag**
string
tailor's chalk, in a pastel color
acrylic tube paint, in cobalt blue
paper plate
1 stencil brush, #4

*We bought ours in an art-supply store.

Procedure:

1. Transfer each of the three stencil designs to the illustration board (see page 15), leaving about 2 inches between designs. Then choose the initials you need from page 198 and transfer them to the same board, making sure that they are positioned next to each other correctly (see the project illustration). Trim the stencil paper so that it is slightly smaller than the illustration board and tape the paper over the three designs—not over

the initials—and cut them out with the X-acto knife. Then, cut them apart, leaving a 1-inch border all around. Center the large diamond stencil directly over the initials and tape it in place. Cut out the initials, peel off the tape, and remove the stencil.

2.   Our bag was designed with several bands of topstitched fabric; because we wanted these to remain unstenciled, we covered them with masking tape, If your bag has bands, do the same; if not, omit this step. Now fill the bag with books, magazines, or newspapers, stretching the fabric as much as possible. This step will ensure that the stenciled designs will be crisp and clear. Next, find the center of the front, back, and two sides of the bag by stretching two pieces of string diagonally from corner to corner; with tailor's chalk, very lightly draw a short vertical line marking each spot at which the strings intersect. Place a strip of masking tape at the center of each side, positioning the tape so that it is on the back half of each side and one edge is flush with the center line. Then, working on the front side of the bag, position the initialed diamond stencil just to the left of the center line, as shown, and tape it into place.

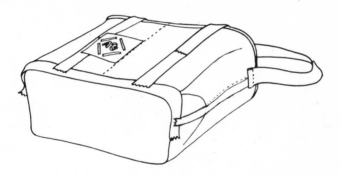

3.   Squeeze a small amount of blue paint onto a paper plate, dip the tip of the brush into the paint, and remove the excess by pouncing the brush on a pile of newspaper. Keeping the edges of the stencil openings pressed down with your fingers, apply the paint through the stencil openings with an up-and-down dabbing motion. When all the openings have been covered with a thin coating of paint, remove the stencil and let the design dry to the touch—a minute or two.

4.   Reposition the stencil so that one side of the stencil's openings fits directly over one side of the image just stenciled, as shown.

In other words, part of the design that you have just stenciled will appear through the repositioned stencil, showing you where the stencil should be taped for the next design. Repeat this procedure over and over again, and the overall pattern will be created for you. Cover the entire front of the bag in this manner, stenciling over the tape when necessary and using the stenciling procedure described in step 3. When you come to a corner of the bag, stencil around the corner and onto the tape that marks the center of the side. When the front and both sides as far as the tape markers have been stenciled, remove the tape and allow the designs to dry. Then reposition both strips of tape so that they are on the front half of the lines indicating the centers of the sides. Starting just to the left of the center line on the back of the bag, repeat the stenciling procedure, continuing around the corners onto the tape markers. Remove the tape when you have completed the stenciling and allow the designs to dry.

5.   Using the same stenciling technique, stencil the small flower design at each intersection above and below the initials, as shown in the illustration.

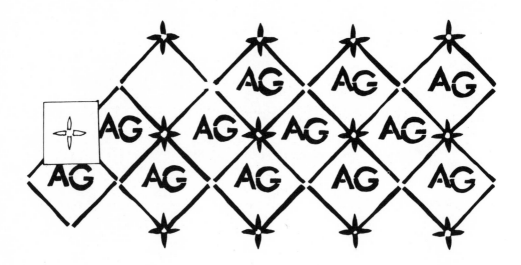

Then stencil the small diamond shape over each of the intersections not stenciled with a flower. The bag is now finished. When the designs are dry, remove the books and peel off the tape covering the fabric strips.

Hints and Ideas:

★Use the same print to adorn other accessories, such as a scarf or a T-shirt, or use just the initials to personalize the pocket of a silk blouse.
★Some other interesting applications of this design are to stencil it on a window shade, the top of an end table, or, if you use japan colors, even on the tiles surrounding your bathtub.

Lotus Blossom T-Shirt

Remember hippies? Those dreamy-eyed exponents of peace, love, and the coming of the Age of Aquarius? They seemed to pose a threat to a self-conscious America that was just emerging from the colorless rigidity of the 1950s. But when it was eventually realized that the cult of flower power was essentially harmless, interested people began to assess the hippie subculture in terms of creative contributions. In fact, the recent surge in the popularity of handicrafts was due in part to all the wonderful things that were sold on the streets of such districts as Haight-Ashbury in San Francisco.

Macramé, weaving, quilting, and ceramics were just a few of the crafts represented at these year-round outdoor fairs. And what sights those bizarre bazaars were! Hippies by the hundreds selling their wares, all dressed in thrift-shop or Renaissance clothes, beribboned, bespangled, and smiling.

It was about this same time that one began to see an abundance of handpainted clothes. Denim jackets and pants, shawls, shoes, and, of course, T-shirts—all were available with handpainted designs ranging from peace symbols to elaborate Lucy-in-the-sky-with-diamonds fantasies.

Because it was so pleasant to see all those gentle rebels in brightly colored clothes, we've included a T-shirt project. Our design is elegantly Oriental and can dress up a basic T to the point of evening wear. Or wear it with jeans for dressed-down chic.

Materials:

washable cotton-knit T-shirt,* in burgundy
3 pieces illustration board, each 15 by 20 inches
scissors
3 sheets stencil paper, each 18 by 24 inches
masking tape
#1 X-acto knife with #11 blades
marking pen
1 piece cardboard, 14 by 18 inches
10 pushpins _or_ thumbtacks
drawing board _or_ plywood piece, at least 18 by 24 inches
tailor's chalk
acrylic tube paints, in turquoise, yellow, and pink
paper plates
3 stencil brushes, all #5
newspaper

*When you use acrylic paint on fabric, you must use a fabric that is washable, since most dry-cleaning fluids will fade or remove acrylic paints.

Procedure:

1. Three different stencil designs are necessary to complete this project. Enlarge each one to size on a separate piece of illustration board (see page 14). Trim the three sheets of stencil paper so that they are slightly smaller than the boards and tape one sheet over each design. Cut the stencils, using a fresh blade in your X-acto knife. Make sure that you cut out the two triangles on each stencil; these are registration marks that will help you to line up your designs on the T-shirt as your stenciling progresses. Now remove the tape holding the stencils to the illustration board, spread the stencils out flat, and label each with a piece of masking tape and a marking pen.

2. To prevent the paint from bleeding through to the back of the T-shirt, slide the piece of cardboard inside the shirt, trimming the cardboard to fit if necessary. Then pin the T-shirt—and the cardboard—to the drawing board with six pushpins, pulling the shirt fairly taut as you pin it.

Stencil A

Each square = 1 inch

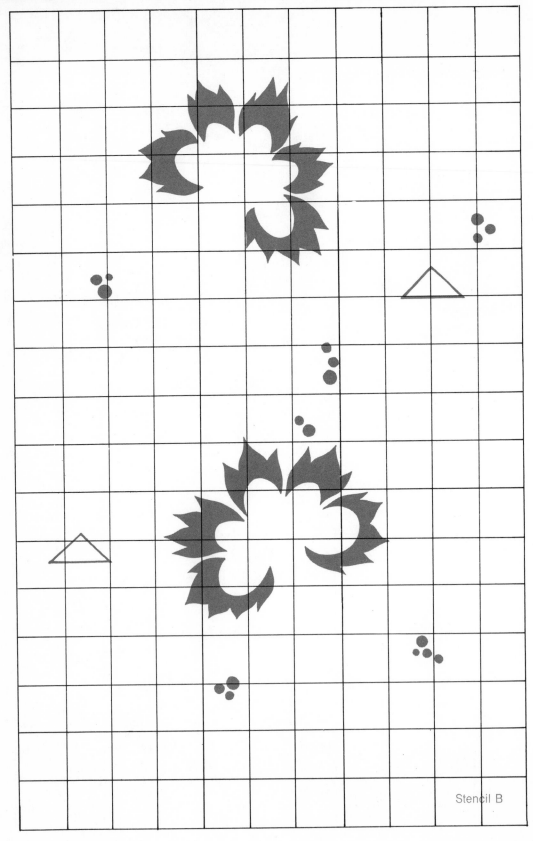

Stencil B

Stencil C

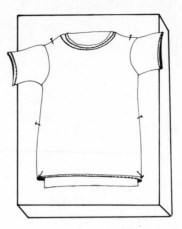

3.   Place stencil A on the front of the T-shirt, making sure that it is well centered and that the bottom of the design touches the lower edge of the T-shirt. Pin it into place with the remaining four pushpins. Outline the registration marks with tailor's chalk by tracing through the two triangles.

4.   Squeeze a small amount of the turquoise acrylic paint onto a paper plate. Dip the tip of a stencil brush into the paint and remove the excess by pouncing the brush on some newspaper. The brush should be fairly dry. Keeping the edges of the stencil openings firmly pressed down with your fingers—on areas so small and intricate that fingers are in the way, try a pencil for this job—apply the paint through the stencil openings. Use an up-and-down dabbing motion and continue to dab until all the openings have been thoroughly coated. Do *not* apply paint through the registration marks; their only purpose is to show you where to place the next stencil. Carefully remove the stencil and allow the paint to dry.

5.   Place stencil B on the T-shirt, taking care that the registration marks are directly over the ones that you made with the tailor's chalk. Pin the stencil in place. Squeeze a small amount of yellow paint onto a second paper plate and dip into it the tip of a clean, dry stencil brush. Remove the excess paint by pouncing the brush on newspaper. Using the same technique that you used with the turquoise paint, apply the paint through the stencil openings. Then remove the stencil and allow the paint to dry.

6. Place stencil C on the T-shirt, making sure that the registration marks are directly over the ones that you made with tailor's chalk; pin the stencil in place. Squeeze a small amount of pink paint onto a paper plate, and, using exactly the same procedures that you did with the previous colors, stencil the design. Carefully remove the stencil and let the design dry; clean your brushes with water.

7. Remove all tacks and the cardboard from the shirt, and remove the chalk marks by rubbing them with a damp sponge. Let the design dry for 48 hours before you wash the T-shirt.

Hints and Ideas:

★If the paint you are stenciling with seems too transparent, leave the stencil in place and apply a second coat after the first coat has dried.
★Stencil the same design on the back of the T-shirt.
★Use these stencils to make an all-over pattern on any washable fabric.

Victorian Satin Sheets and Pillowcases

As twilight deepened, we were sipping martinis in the club car of a train that was steadily making its way from California to New York. It had been an especially successful trip, and we were treating ourselves to a slow, scenic ride on the last of those luxury trains once famous for trans-continental elegance.

Suddenly, something like a barking telephone book whizzed across the table, demolishing crystal glasses and ashtrays. Startled, wet, and covered with a fine layer of cigarette ash, we leaped to our feet only to be surprised a second time. Before us was a tall, shawl-shrouded figure with a thick mane of flaming red hair. After glaring at us disdainfully for a moment, she pushed us aside, scooped up the now-docile dog, and stalked from the car.

A porter scuttled up and began trying to dry us off. The chilling apparition had been, he informed us, the famous actress, Mrs. _____ de la _____. Once the toast of two continents, she was now in her twilight years.

Later that evening, the same porter approached us once again, this time with a small silver platter bearing a cream-colored card. On it was written: "You will come and bid Tante _____ good night."

As we entered her compartment, we were amazed at its lavishness. Bud vases with fresh roses were bracketed to the walls, and the silver frames of dozens of sepia photographs gleamed from all around. Volumes of leather-bound scripts were stacked everywhere. In the midst of the splendor was Mrs. _____ de la _____, reclining upon a mountainous bed covered with lustrous, white satin sheets. At one point in the monologue that followed—even though her legendary beauty had faded, we sat, listened, and stared—she mentioned that her sheets always traveled with her. Even the finest cotton, she said, was abrasive to her delicate, patrician skin.

Unfortunately, we didn't see Mrs. _____ de la _____ again during the trip. Our notes came back unanswered. Outside Grand Central Station, as we were loading our new acquisitions into a taxi, a horn blasted behind us. We jumped to the curb as a gigantic old limousine sped past. From deep within its recesses, a thin hand waved languidly. Had it not been for a flash of flame-colored hair, we wouldn't have known who it was.

Materials:
1 set polyester-satin sheets,* in any size, in maroon
1 set polyester-satin pillowcases, in standard size, in maroon
1 piece illustration board, 20 by 30 inches
scissors
2 sheets stencil paper, each 18 by 24 inches
masking tape
#1 X-acto knife with #11 blades
marking pen
iron
newspaper
yardstick
tailor's chalk
acrylic tube paints, in light peach and moss green
paper plates
2 stencil brushes, both #5

*Since dry-cleaning fluids will fade or remove acrylic paints from fabric, you must choose sheets and pillowcases that are washable or else substitute textile paints for the acrylics. Even though we have called for a set of sheets, you will be stenciling only the topsheet.

Procedure:

1. Enlarge each of the stencil designs to size on the illustration board (see page 14), allowing at least 2 inches of space between designs. Also choose from the stencil alphabet given on page 199 the two initials you need, and enlarge them on the same board. Cut one of the sheets of stencil paper in half and tape the two halves over design A; tape the other sheet over the remaining designs. Using the X-acto knife, cut the stencils and then cut around the stencils, leaving at least a 1-inch border all around. Separate the two stencils cut from design A, turn one of them over, and label them A-1 and A-2, using masking tape and a marking pen.

Each square = 1 inch

Stencil A

Stencil B

Stencil C

2.   Using an iron set for synthetics, press the topsheet and both pillow-cases until they are flat and wrinkle-free. Using the yardstick and tailor's chalk, draw lines that divide each pillowcase into quarters. Then cover a large work surface with several layers of newspaper. Spread one of the pillowcases out flat on the newspaper and slide several layers of news-paper inside the pillowcase to prevent the paint from bleeding through the back side; prepare the other pillowcase in the same way.

3.   Tape stencil A-1 to one pillowcase, making sure that both edges of the design just touch the guidelines, as shown.

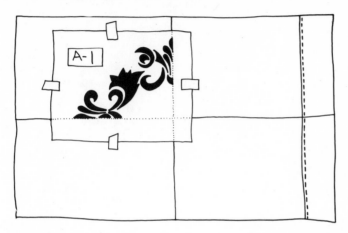

Squeeze a small amount of peach paint onto a paper plate, dip the tip of a stencil brush into the paint, and remove the excess by pouncing the bristles on some newspapers. Begin to stencil by gently dabbing the color through the stencil openings. Use an up-and-down dabbing motion to apply the color, and work from the outside edges toward the center. When all the openings have been filled with color, carefully lift the stencil straight up and off the pillowcase.

4.   Reposition the same stencil as shown, taking care that the edges of the design touch the guidelines.

Tape the stencil in place, dab the color through the openings, and carefully lift off the stencil when all the openings have been filled.

5.   Position stencil A-2 as shown, again aligning the edges of the design with the guidelines.

Tape the stencil in place, dab on the color, and carefully lift off the stencil.

6.   To complete the border on the pillowcase, reposition stencil A-2, placing the edges of the design on the guidelines.

Tape the stencil in place, dab on the paint, and lift off the stencil when finished.

7.   To stencil the second pillowcase, repeat steps 3 through 6.

8.   Now, lay the sheet right side up on your work surface. Find the center of its width and, using the tailor's chalk, mark it at several points along its

length. Center the yardstick over the marks and draw a vertical guideline on each side of the yardstick. Next, draw a horizontal guideline 9 inches below and parallel to the top edge of the sheet.

9.   Position stencil B as shown, making sure that the top and bottom stencil openings fit up against the vertical guideline on the right and that the horizontal guideline runs straight through the center of the design.

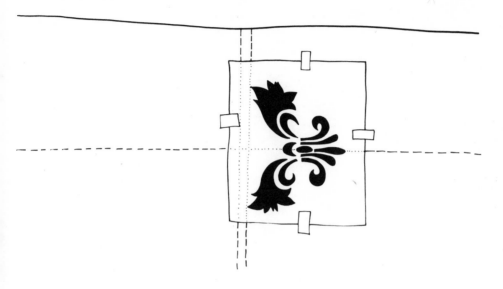

Then tape the stencil in place. Using the same peach shade and brush, apply the color through the stencil openings and then lift off the stencil.

10.   Turn the same stencil around (do not turn it over because the paint will still be wet) and position it as shown.

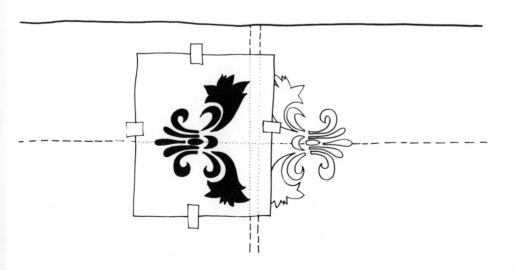

This time the top and bottom of the stencil design should touch the vertical guideline on the left. Again, the horizontal guideline should run through the center of the design. Tape the design in place, apply the paint, and remove the stencil carefully.

11.   Position stencil C as shown, making sure that the horizontal guideline runs through the center of the design.

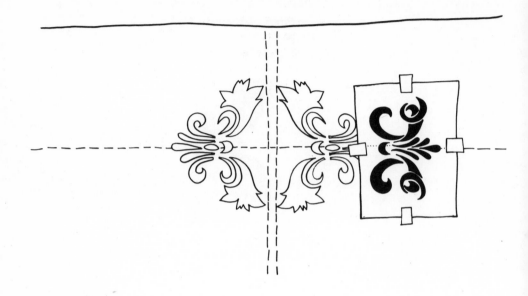

Tape the stencil in place, apply the paint, and then carefully remove the stencil.

12.   Turn the same stencil around and position it as shown.

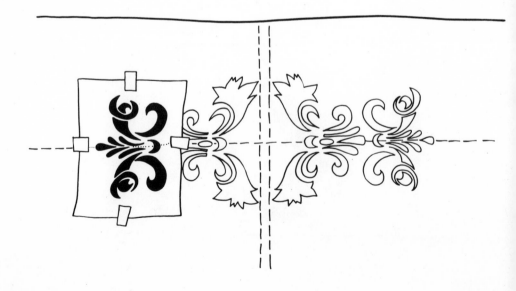

Tape it in place, stencil on the color, and then remove the stencil. The sheet border is now finished.

13.   Now stencil the initials onto the pillowcases. Using the chalk guidelines to center them, position the initials as shown.

Tape them in place. Squeeze a small amount of green paint onto a clean paper plate and, using a clean, dry brush, apply the color. When all the openings have been filled, remove the stencil. Repeat this procedure on the other pillowcase.

14.   All the stenciling is now completed. Clean your brushes with water and paper towels. After the paint is thoroughly dry (several hours), remove the tailor's chalk by wiping it off with a slightly moistened sponge.

Hints and Ideas:

★If you are handy with a sewing machine, try sewing your own satin sheets instead of buying them. Not only will you save money, but you will be able to find a wider range of colors, since nearly every large fabric house carries a good selection of polyester satins.

★Stencil this design on polyester-cotton bedsheets, or use it to glamorize a set of bath towels.

★If you are stenciling a light design on dark satin, as we did, you may need to give each design a second coat of paint. If so, let the first coat dry with the stencil in place and then apply the second coat. Two coats will make the design stand out more, providing more contrast.

Choose an absorbent paper; avoid shiny or metallic papers unless you use a pen specially designed for them. Various coloring media can be used on paper; unless otherwise noted, final designs require no further protection. *Acrylics* can be used on paper, cardboard, or illustration board for permanent de-sign signs; use a stencil brush. *Colored pencils* work especially well on textured papers: Start with light colors and build intensity. Spray-ing workable fixative over the design will enable you to go over it again and again without smudging. Spray the final design with a mat fixative. *Inks* are best applied with a sponge strip. Always test for permanence; if the ink is nonpermanent, spray the final design with a mat fixative. *Marking pens, nonpermanent,* work well on all absorbent papers. Test colors on paper scraps. We prefer pens with fat, soft tips. Since inks are transparent, work on light-colored papers. Experiment with textures: crosshatch, stroke diagonally, use small dots. Before changing colors, blot the stencil with a damp sponge and let dry. Protect the finished design with several light coats of spray fixative. Sheets of clear, self-adhesive plastic can also be placed over designs. *Marking pens, permanent,* are good for designs that may be exposed to moisture. To counteract "bleeding," work quickly or use old marking pens—the ink bleeds most when the pen is new. *Poster paints* are water-based, nonpermanent paints that are good for stenciling on almost any kind of paper. Use a stencil brush, watercolor brush, or sponge strip. If you're stenciling on shiny paper and the paint "resists," add a few drops of liquid detergent. Protect the final design with spray fixative; or, use varnish or shellac after first mounting the design on illustration board to prevent it from curling as it dries. *Watercolors* can be stenciled on all absorbent papers. Use a watercolor brush or a sponge strip; stencil with a fairly dry brush. Protect the final design with spray fixative.

Americana Pantry Labels

It was the height of peach season, and Jim B. was driving back from a vacation in Canada. Stopping at a roadside stand at the base of a shady tree, he bought a big lug of peaches for an unbelievably low price. They were the best he'd ever had, and even though he gorged himself for the rest of the ride, there still seemed to be hundreds left when he reached Manhattan.

Overpeached, he appealed to friends, who persuaded him to try his hand at home canning. Armed with a batch of recipes and a big box overflowing with hardware and assorted paraphenalia, he went to the kitchen to immortalize the flavor of those high-summer peaches. The kitchen was soon a disaster area, but the resulting preserves were unquestionably blue-ribbon quality. Proud of what he'd done (and tired of peaches), he decided to give the preserves as Christmas gifts. Because it was impossible to find labels that did justice to his creation, he decided to make his own.

To combat the scarcity of attractive labels, we've designed three that are versatile enough to put on almost anything. Stenciled labels will enhance homemade as well as store-bought foodstuffs and will make your pantry look like a treasure trove of rare, savory delicacies. They take only a few minutes to do, and one stencil will enable you to make enough labels to personalize as many containers of goodies as you wish.

Materials:

1 piece illustration board, 15 by 20 inches
scissors
1 sheet stencil paper, 18 by 24 inches
masking tape
#1 X-acto knife with #11 blades
straight pin
paper punch
construction paper, in white *or* light colors
felt-tipped markers,* in bright colors of your choice
pencil
white glue

*Except for the fact that indelible felt-tipped pens tend to bleed when they are new, this type of pen is probably your best choice for this project. If your pens are not indelible, protect the finished labels by spraying them with fixative, which is only partly permanent; brushing them with clear lacquer or polyurethane; or covering them with transparent pressure-sensitive plastic.

Procedure:

1. Enlarge to size as many of the label designs as you wish to make on the illustration board (see page 14), trim the stencil paper slightly smaller than the illustration board, and tape it in place over the designs. Using the X-acto knife, cut out all the inner designs except for the small circles. To do these, first make a hole in the center of each with a straight pin. Next, cut out each of the stencils on the dotted lines.

Each square = 1 inch

Finally, using a paper punch, punch out each circle, centering the punch over each pinhole.

2. Using the stencils, pens of several different colors, and scraps of paper, experiment with various color combinations—you'll notice that the colors show up best on white or light backgrounds—and practice the stenciling technique. Keeping the edges of the stencil openings firmly pressed down with your fingers—they should be pressing the areas that you are stenciling and then moved along as you continue to work—practice outlining the design by tracing through stencil openings and then filling in with color. To avoid overworking the paper, fill in the color quickly and evenly; torn or scruffy paper may result if you color over the designs more than a few times.

3. When you have chosen your color scheme and have perfected the technique, place one stencil design over a piece of construction paper cut just slightly larger than the design and fill in the openings, holding the stencil firmly in place. Then outline the label with a pencil, as shown.

Cut out the label with scissors, following the pencil outline.

4. To attach the label to a jar, cover the back of the label with a thin coat of glue and let it dry until it is slightly sticky. Press it into place on a clean, dry jar, holding it firmly until it begins to adhere. If the glue does not form a bond, apply another thin coat and try again. Let the glue dry thoroughly.

5. Repeat step 3 to make the other two label designs.

Hints and Ideas:
★Use these stencils to make labels for file cabinets, sewing boxes, or canisters, or use them to make place cards or notecards.

Art Nouveau Stationery and Envelopes

With stencils, you can design your own distinctive stationery and envelopes in no time at all. You can even create stationery to match your every mood —stencil a love letter with a garland of intertwining hearts and flowers or decorate a "Dear John" letter with bittersweet bouquets of forget-me-nots. You can even dress up a business letter to really get your point across.

We chose an Art Nouveau border for this project, but inspiration for a design that's "really you" can come from many places. You may come upon the perfect thing while leafing through a magazine, for instance. If you've read Chapter 1, you know how easy it is to make a stencil of that design. And once you've made the stencil, you can quickly turn almost any sheet of paper into a lovely, unique piece of stationery.

Remember to experiment with colors as you stencil. We used a pale blue paper that contrasted nicely with the deep blue border, but lemon yellow paper with a fresh green border would also be striking. After you try this project, begin to build a collection of stationery stencils to choose from. If you have a wide selection, you'll always be letter-perfect.

Materials:

paper and envelopes, both standard business size, in pale blue
1 piece illustration board, 15 by 20 inches
scissors
1 sheet stencil paper, 18 by 24 inches
masking tape
#1 X-acto knife with #11 blades
newspaper
4 straight pins (optional)
waterproof ink, in dark blue
small household sponge, cut into 1-inch strips

Procedure:

1. Enlarge both stencil designs to size on the illustration board (see page 14), leaving at least 2 inches of space between them. Cut the stencil paper slightly smaller than the illustration board and tape it in place over the designs. Using the X-acto knife, cut the stencils, taking care not to sever the bridges that hold the stencils together (see page 19 for stencil repair). This set of designs is especially delicate, so it's important that you cut slowly and accurately. To make the long cuts that curve around corners, remove the knife when you reach a curve, shift the board to a more comfortable position, and then resume cutting after carefully replacing your knife in the cut. When you have finished cutting the designs, cut them apart, leaving at least a 1-inch border all around.

2. Cover your work surface with a layer of newspaper and lay the illustration board face down on top. Place a piece of stationery on the board, and position the stencil on top, making sure that the space around the edges of the design is equal on all four sides. If you wish, insert straight pins through all four corners to hold the stencil and stationery in place as you work.

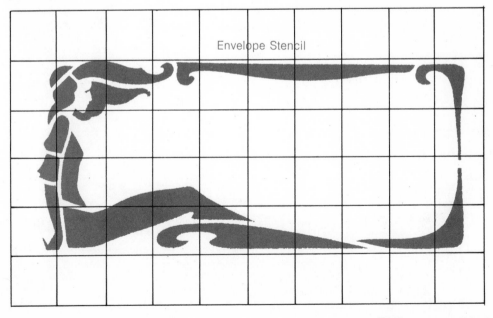

Envelope Stencil

Each square = 1 inch

Stationery Stencil

Each square = 1 inch

3. Pour about a tablespoon of ink into a saucer. Holding one of the strips of sponge as you would a pencil, dip the tip into the ink.

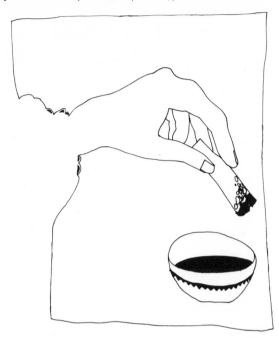

When the tip is thoroughly moistened, pounce it on some newspaper to remove the excess ink—too much ink on the sponge will result in a wet, messy design. Begin stenciling by dabbing the sponge through the stencil openings, using an up-and-down motion; don't brush or stroke. When all the openings have been filled with color, let the stationery dry for a minute or two. Then carefully lift the stencil straight up. You should be rewarded with a beautifully crisp image.

4. To stencil the envelope, follow the same procedure outlined in steps 2 and 3, but use the rectangular stencil instead of the one designed for the stationery.

Hints and Ideas:

★If the stationery warps after it has been stenciled, just iron it flat when it is dry.

★If you have used too much ink while stenciling, the ink may "bead up" on the stencil. Before stenciling the next piece of stationery, gently blot the stencil with a paper towel or tissue.

Madame Moon's Luminaries

A few years ago, traveling through the Southwest researching American Indian designs, we were introduced to a singular Oriental woman, Madame Moon, who reportedly owned one of the finest collections of native ceramic sculpture in the area. After many conversations with this grand old lady, we were finally extended an invitation to view her collection.

On the appointed evening, we hired a driver to take us to her sprawling adobe hacienda, built atop a long, low mesa. As we alighted from the car, the only sounds we heard were the tinkling of bells in the trees and the rush of running water. We passed through an opening in a high, thick wall of living cactus and were met by an unbelievable sight. As we stood at the foot of the mesa, the house, as well as the winding stone stairway that led to it, appeared to be a giant, sparkling jewel, a luminous opal alive with light.

When we reached the stairs, we discovered the secret of this fabulous illusion. All along the stairway were hundreds of glowing paper bags; they outlined terraces and ledges and even framed a rock-lined pool. Each bag, weighted with sand and containing a burning candle, was emblazoned with an Oriental design. The hospitable Madame Moon called her magic lanterns "luminaries."

Stenciling paper bags and turning them into luminaries is one of the quickest, easiest ways to transform an ordinary patio into a shimmering scene for a late-night garden party. Or to set the mood for a long, lazy evening on the beach. One thing is for sure: Wherever you use these magical luminaries, you're bound to create romance.

Materials:
brown paper bags, each at least 7 by 10½ inches
1 piece illustration board, 15 by 20 inches
scissors
1 sheet stencil paper, 18 by 24 inches
masking tape
#1 X-acto knife with #11 blades
newspaper
iron (optional)
waterproof india ink, in black
small household sponge, cut into 1-inch strips
sand *or* gravel *or* soil
dripless utility candles

Procedure:
1. Enlarge the stencil design to size on the center of the illustration board (see page 14). Trim the stencil paper slightly smaller than the illustration board and tape it in place over the design. Using the X-acto knife, cut the stencil slowly and accurately, taking care not to sever any of the bridges (see page 19 for stencil repair). Because the design is relatively intricate and somewhat circular, it is best to keep shifting the board so that you will always be moving the knife toward yourself. When you have finished cutting the stencil, cut around it, leaving at least a 1-inch border all around.

2. Spread a layer of newspaper over your work surface, making sure that the newspaper is flat. Press it with a hot iron if necessary. Fold one of the paper bags as flat as possible; if necessary, press the bag with a hot iron to flatten it further and to eliminate any wrinkles. Finally, center the stencil design on top of the bag.

3. Pour a small amount of ink into a saucer. Holding one of the strips of sponge as you would a pencil, dip the end of the sponge into the ink. When the tip is moist and soft, pounce it on a stack of newspaper to remove excess ink. If too much ink remains on the sponge, the edges of the stenciled design will be fuzzy. Holding the design in place on the bag with your fingers, begin stenciling by gently dabbing the tip of the sponge up and down through the stencil openings.

Each square = 1 inch

Continue dabbing until all the openings have been coated with color. You will find that the ink does not always go on evenly, but this unevenness adds to the rustic charm of the piece and enhances its handmade look. However, if you wish a more even effect, dip the sponge back into the ink, pounce the tip, and restencil the more faded areas. Let the design dry for a moment and then carefully lift the stencil straight up.

4. Repeat steps 2 and 3 to make as many luminaries as you wish.

5. After the bags are all stenciled and the ink is dry, unfold the bags and stand them up. To weight the bags and keep them stationary, fill each of them about one-quarter full of sand, gravel, or soil. Place a candle inside each bag, pushing it into the sand until it touches the bottom of the bag. All that remains to be done is the lighting of the candles and the beginning of the music. Be sure to pick a still, windless day on which to use your luminaries.

Hints and Ideas:

★These stenciled bags can attractively house a picnic lunch. They are also a great gift-wrap idea.

★Use the dragon stencil on the front of a T-shirt, using acrylic paint.

Nefertiti Notecards and Envelopes

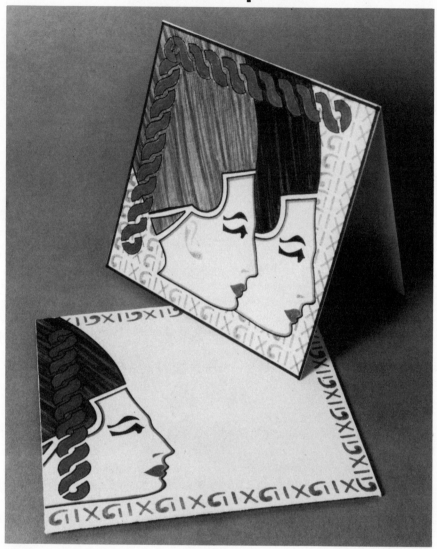

Instead of sending a card with someone else's message on it, try this project, compose your own sentiment, and then branch out into your own visual experimentation. It would be impossible to list here all the possibilities presented by notecards. Suffice it to say that there are twelve months in the year, and in those twelve months there are holidays, seasonal themes, family celebrations, and other thinking-of-you times that can be translated into fantastic stencil graphics.

This particular card features two profiles of a regal queen; for an even more personal touch, use a profile photo of a friend, relative, or yourself to make your stencil design.

Materials:

1 piece illustration board, 15 by 20 inches
scissors
1 sheet stencil paper, 18 by 24 inches
masking tape
#1 X-acto knife with #11 blades
ruler
pencil
3 sheets construction paper, each 18 by 24 inches, one in white and
    two in beige
1 fine-point nonpermanent marking pen, in black
5 broad-tipped nonpermanent marking pens, in red, blue, black, orange,
    and light brown
white glue

Procedure:

1.   This project involves the technique of overlapping, which produces a
tight, compact design that plays down the fact that stencils were used to
achieve it. It's a very easy technique but one that should be experimented
with first. For example, say that you have cut a circular design that you wish
to stencil by overlapping. First, stencil the circle and fill it in with a dark
color (Figure A in the illustration). Place the same stencil over but slightly

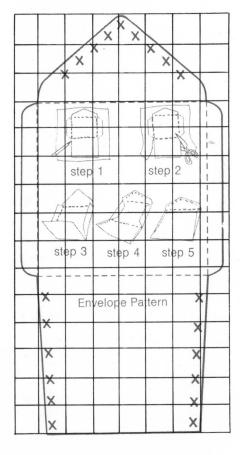

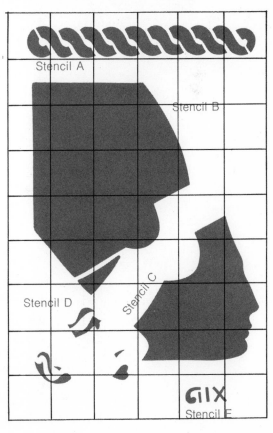

Each square = 1 inch

to the right of the circle you just stenciled so that part of the previously stenciled circle shows through the opening. As you begin to trace the second circle (Figure B in the illustration), start the line at the edge of the darkened circle and continue it around the opening until you reach the darkened circle again. When you lift off the stencil, you will have an over-lapped design, with the first circle stenciled appearing to overlap the second (Figure C in the illustration).

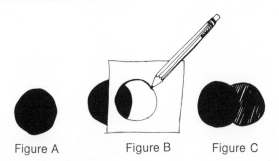

Figure A   Figure B   Figure C

2.   To stencil the notecard, enlarge the five stencil designs to size on the illustration board (see page 14), leaving at least 2 inches of space between designs. Trim the stencil paper to a size slightly smaller than the illustration board and tape it in place over the designs. Using the X-acto knife, cut the stencils and then cut around them, leaving at least a 1-inch border all around. Label each stencil with a piece of masking tape and a marking pen.

3.   Using a ruler and a pencil, draw a rectangle that measures 6 by 12 inches on one of the sheets of beige construction paper. Cut it out with the scissors and fold it in half so that you have a 6-inch square. Position stencil A along the fold of the notecard, moving it about ¼ inch down from the top and about ¼ inch in from the left-hand side. Holding the stencil down firmly with one hand, use the red marker to fill in all the openings. Still holding the stencil firmly in place, outline the red designs with the fine black pen. Reposition stencil A along the left-hand side of the card, leaving a ¼-inch margin along the side and overlapping the design at the top, as shown.

Fill in the stencil openings with the red marker and then outline them with the fine black marker.

4.   Position stencil B so that the upper left-hand corner of the stencil conforms with the upper left-hand corner of the notecard.

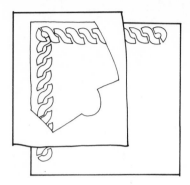

Keeping the stencil firmly in place, fill in the stencil openings with the blue marker. Since marking pens often leave streaks when applied to large areas, always stroke in the same direction. The streaks will then look professional rather than sloppy. As you color around the red rope design, take particular care not to get the blue on the red. After the stencil openings have been completely filled in with blue, keep the stencil in place and stencil a thin black line around the blue shape.

5.   Position stencil C close to the blue crown, separating it by about ⅛ inch.

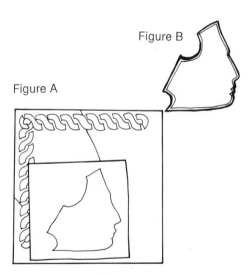

Figure B

Figure A

Holding the stencil firmly in place, outline the face with the orange pen (Figure A in the illustration). Using the fine black marker, add another outline around the face (Figure B in the illustration).

6.   Now move stencil C to the right, as shown, so that it partially overlaps the face just stenciled.

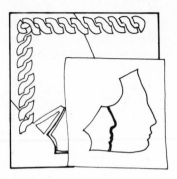

Holding it firmly in place, outline it again in orange and then black, using the same procedures you used in step 5. Take care that the outlines stop at the edge of the face you just stenciled.

7.   Position stencil B as shown, fitting it close to the face but separating it by about ⅛ inch.

Fill the crown in with black, taking care not to apply color onto any of the previously stenciled sections that appear through the openings.

8.   Place stencil D inside the face, as shown. The outline of the face will show through the stencil (indicated by the dotted line) for easy positioning. Color in the eye with black, the mouth with red, and the ear with light brown.

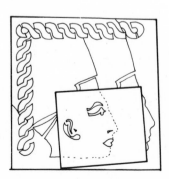

9.   Move stencil D to the right, positioning it inside the face on the right. Fill in the eye with black and the mouth with red. When you have removed the stencil, the two faces should look like this.

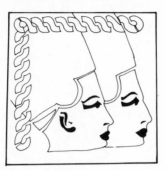

10.   Use stencil E to fill in the background around the heads and woven designs. Begin stenciling on the left and use the light brown marker for color. As you complete the filling in, keep repositioning the design so that an overall pattern is formed, as shown.

When the background is completely filled in, the notecard is finished.

11.   To make the matching envelope for your notecard, enlarge the envelope pattern on the sheet of white construction paper (see page 14) and cut it out with the scissors. Lay the pattern on the second sheet of beige construction paper and, holding it in place, trace around it; then cut it out. Save the pattern for making other envelopes. Look at the illustration to see how the envelope should look when stenciled.

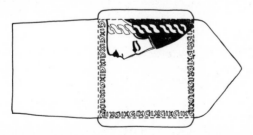

Using the same stenciling procedure that you did for the notecard, stencil the envelope. Use stencils A through E in alphabetical order. Finally, fold the envelope into shape and glue it, following the figures shown on the envelope pattern.

Every-Occasion Gift Wrap

Have you noticed that gift wrap seems to get more expensive every year? And that the hollow cardboard tubes inside the wrapping paper seem to get larger? Besides the problem of expense, it's often difficult to find gift wrap that is special enough for a favorite relative or friend. With stencils, you can create an endless assortment of meaningful designs while saving yourself a small fortune.

Our design, a little peasant girl bearing a huge bouquet of wildflowers, is general enough to fit any occasion. But our design should be only the beginning of your adventure into custom gift wrap. Make up your own designs, use one from another of our projects, or simply spray paint over a flower, a leaf, or a doily.

Materials:

gift box, approximately 7 by 7 by 11 inches
roll of inexpensive wrapping paper,* in white
1 piece illustration board, 15 by 20 inches
scissors
1 sheet stencil paper, 18 by 24 inches
masking tape
pencil
transparent tape
#1 X-acto knife with #11 blades
nonpermanent marking pen, in green

*Some possibilities are butcher's paper, drawing paper, wrapping paper, and shelf paper.

Procedure:

1. Enlarge the two stencil designs to size on the illustration board (see page 14), leaving at least 2 inches of space between designs. Trim the

Each square = 1 inch

stencil paper so that it is slightly smaller in size than the illustration board, and tape it in place over the designs. Cut the stencils with the X-acto knife and then cut around each, allowing a 1-inch margin all around.

2.   Begin by rolling out a length of paper; set the box on its side on top, and, holding it stationary with one hand, trace around it with a pencil. Turn the box over onto its next side and trace around that. In the same way, trace around the third and fourth sides of the box, as shown in the illustration.

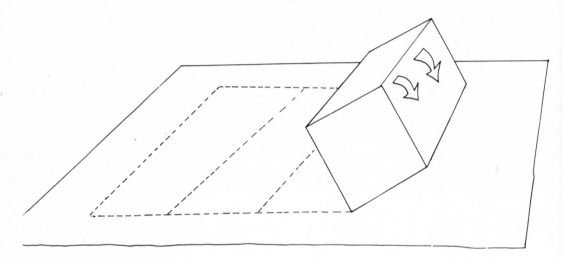

3.   Position the stencils on the wrapping paper as shown in the illustration.

Make sure that each design is within the lines that you have traced, and then tape the stencils into place. In order to prevent marring the paper that will be wrapped around the box, keep the tape *outside* the traced lines. Using the green marking pen, stencil the designs, and then remove the stencils.

4.   Lay out another section of wrapping paper and make tracings of the top and the bottom of the box on it. Add an extension around each, as shown in Figure A of the illustration, and cut the pieces out with scissors.

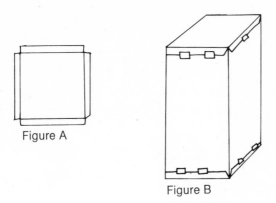

Figure A

Figure B

Attach these sections to the top and bottom of the box with transparent tape, as shown in Figure B of the illustration above.

5.   Finally, cut out the stenciled gift wrap with scissors, following the outside pencil line that defines the large rectangle. Fold the paper along the pencil lines that remain within the rectangle and then erase the lines. Wrap the paper around the box, as shown, and fasten it with tape at the back.

The gift is ready to be tied up with ribbon.

Hints and Ideas:

★Make a matching card by utilizing one or both of these designs.

★Instead of using just one color of marking pen to make a monochromatic design, use a variety of brightly colored marking pens.

★For unusual and inexpensive gift wrap, stencil on old newspaper.

Stencilman Kite

Kites are fun. These silent sky machines are fun to make and exhilarating to fly, no matter what your age. We've designed ours with a superhero motif, but almost any design, whether from this book or one you make up, can be adapted to fit a paper kite. And the next time somebody tells you to go fly a kite, take his advice.

Materials:

paper kite, at least 24 by 30 inches, in white
1 piece illustration board, 20 by 30 inches
2 sheets stencil paper, each 18 by 24 inches
transparent tape
scissors
masking tape
#1 X-acto knife with #11 blades
4 large paper clips
nonpermanent marking pens, in assorted colors

Procedure:

1.   Enlarge the stencil design to size on the illustration board (see page 14). Then place the two sheets of stencil paper side by side to make a

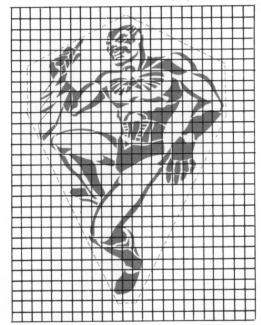

Each square = 1 inch

rectangle that measures 24 by 36 inches. Fit the two sheets together as closely as possible without overlapping them, and join the seam with the transparent tape. Turn the paper over and tape the seam on the back, too. Then trim the paper so that it is slightly smaller than the illustration board, and tape it over the design with masking tape. Using the X-acto knife, cut out the stencil. Finally, cut around the stencil on the dotted line.

2.   Position the stencil over the kite and then paper-clip it into place. At this point, the kite is ready to be stenciled. You can either color it yourself or give it to a group of children to color. Since any color scheme will work, you can approach this project as you would a coloring book— that's part of the fun. Just remember that as you are stenciling, one hand should be holding the marker and the other hand should be pressing down the edges of the stencil openings next to the sections being filled in. When all the areas have been colored, remove the stencil and the kite is ready to fly.

3

Food

Food stencils appear most appealing when applied to a smooth surface. After rolling out cookie or pie-crust dough, choose the smoother side for stenciling; when placing bread dough in the baking pan, place the smoothest side up. Brownies or cakes should be inverted to place the smooth side up. Pies and cookies are stenciled on flat, un-baked dough; brownies, breads, and cakes are stenciled after baking. For cookies, choose a shortbread recipe that won't spread while baking. If you're stenciling a frosted cake with con-fectioners sugar, make sure the frosting is as smooth as possible and let it "set" before sten-ciling. Food coloring can be mixed with a small amount of water and used on cookie or pie-crust dough. Use a small watercolor brush or a sponge strip; an airbrush will also work. Food paint is a mixture of egg yolk, water, and food coloring. It produces a rich, glazed effect and gives your creation a "finished" look. Food coloring alone may "resist" on certain doughs, but food paint will adhere in these cases. Stencil with a small watercolor brush. Both food coloring and food paint are transpar-ent; it's therefore best to start with light col-ors and build up to dark-er ones. Bits of food—for instance, minced red and green cherries, colored sugar, candy bits, chocolate shot, shredded coconut, candied fruit bits, grated milk choco-late, silver dragées, sifted confectioners sugar, cinnamon hearts, sifted cocoa, raisins, nuts, sunflower seeds, black olive bits, pick-le relish, chopped pimiento, poppy seeds, sesame seeds, caviar, sieved hard-cooked eggs, bits of green or red pep-pers—can be used to sten-cil foods. Use these items on frosted cakes, canapés that have been spread with a savory but-ter, or a sandwich loaf that has been spread with softened cream cheese. Allow the frosting, but-ter, or cream cheese to almost set before sten-ciling. Then gently press the bits into the surface, carefully remove the sten-cil, and allow the sur-face to set completely.

Fleur-de-Lis Loaf

Add a subtly elegant touch to any meal with this fresh loaf of bread emblazoned with a sprinkling of fleur-de-lis. Breads offer many possibilities for stenciled designs. Bake a batch of rolls and then stencil a rosebud on the top of each. If you're serving international cuisine, choose an appropriate bread and stencil it with a motif that symbolizes the nationality of the meal.

The recipe we've included for this project makes two delicious loaves of bread. As long as you're making one, you may as well make an extra to freeze for a later occasion. If you don't want to bake your own, try this design on bakery bread or on prepared, refrigerated bread dough, which is available in most grocery stores.

Materials:
loaf of unsliced white bread (recipe follows)
1 piece illustration board, 4 inches square
masking tape
1 piece stencil paper, 3 inches square
#1 X-acto knife with #11 blades
1 egg yolk
food coloring, in red, yellow, and blue
1 watercolor brush, #3

Procedure:

1.   Because bread changes its shape during baking, it is always stenciled after it has been baked. It should be stenciled when either slightly warm or cool, never hot. Here's our favorite bread recipe.

Favorite Bread Recipe

2 packages active dry yeast	1 tablespoon salt
1 cup warm water (110° F.)	⅓ cup sugar
½ cup vegetable shortening	8 to 8½ cups all-purpose flour
2 cups buttermilk	

Soften the yeast in the warm water. Melt the shortening in a metal cup and let it cool till lukewarm. Place the buttermilk in a large bowl along with the yeast mixture, shortening, salt, and sugar; mix well. Add 2 cups of flour; beat well. Add enough of the remaining flour to make a moderately stiff dough. Place it on a floured board and knead it until very smooth (8 to 10 minutes). Shape it into a ball and place it in a greased bowl, turning it once to grease the top; leave it in a warm place (80° to 85° F.) for 1¼ hours, or until it has doubled in bulk. Punch down the dough, form it into a ball, and let it rest for 10 minutes. Shape it into two loaves and place each in a greased 9 × 5 × 3-inch bread pan; return the pans to a warm place and let the dough rise for 45 minutes. Bake the loaves in a preheated 400° F. oven for 35 minutes, or until done. Immediately remove the loaves from the pans and cool them on racks. Makes two loaves. Note: If the tops brown too quickly, cover them loosely with aluminum foil during the last 15 minutes of baking.

2.   Transfer the stencil design to the piece of illustration board (see page

15), and tape the stencil paper over the design. Using the X-acto knife, cut the stencil.

3.　To stencil this project, you will need a base mixture of egg yolk and water to which food color is added. To make the base, place half an egg yolk (save the other half for stenciling other breads) in a cup along with ½ teaspoon of water. Add 6 drops of red food coloring and 6 drops of yellow food coloring; mix well. Blend in one drop of blue food coloring to make the desired shade of brown.

4.　Place the stencil in one corner of the top of the loaf of bread. Dip the tip of the brush into the food paint, and remove the excess color from the brush by gently pressing the bristles against the side of the cup. Begin to stencil by tracing around the inside edge of the stencil opening to outline the design; then fill in the design with more food paint until the design is evenly coated with color. Your designs may need two coats of color; if so, let the first coat dry before applying the second.

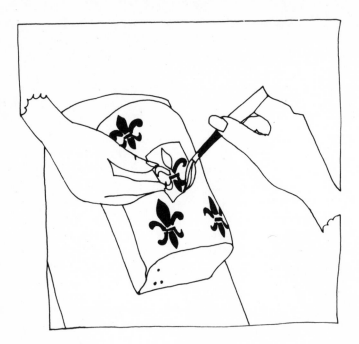

5.　While the first design is drying, reposition the stencil in one of the corners at the opposite end of the loaf. Using the same stenciling procedure described in step 4, stencil the fleur-de-lis. Repeat in all four corners of the top and once in the center of the loaf. Allow the designs to dry before serving the bread.

Hints and Ideas:

★Stenciled breads can be frozen for several months if they are wrapped airtight.

★Stencil a name across the top of your bread, using the letter stencils given for the Message Cookies on page 117.

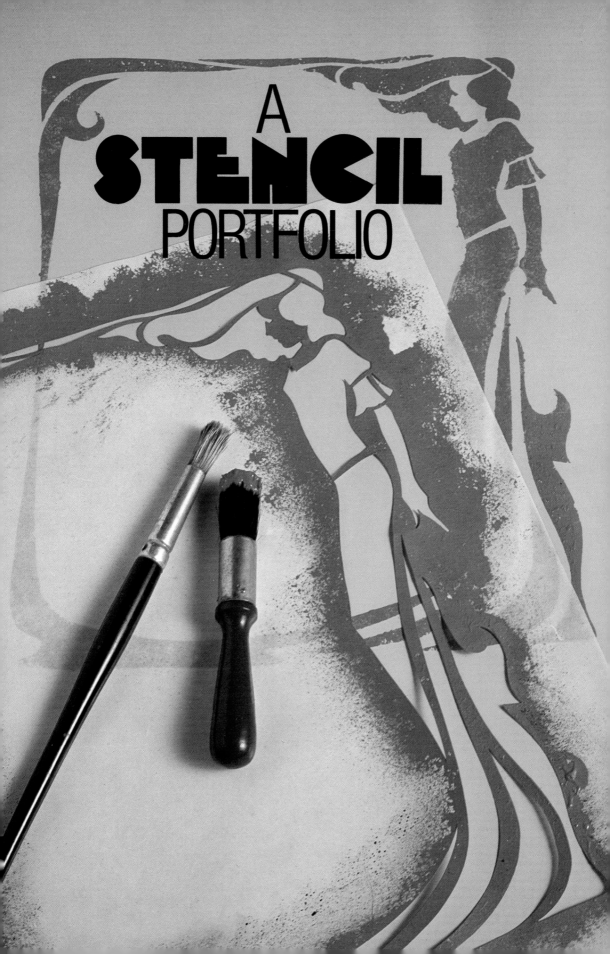

A STENCIL PORTFOLIO

Above: Every-Occasion Gift Wrap, page 86. *Right:* Heavenly Huge Hopscotch, page 184.

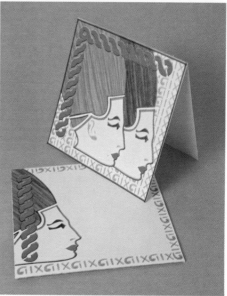

Top: Art Deco Auto, page 175. *Left:* Stencil-man Kite, page 90. *Above:* Nefertiti Notecards and Envelopes, page 80.

Preceding pages (clockwise from upper left): Celebration Cake, page 121; Well-Dressed Turkey, page 105; Picture-Perfect Pie, page 110; Message Cookies, page 115; Garden Party Sandwiches, page 125; Sugar-Sifted Brownies, page 118; Fleur-de-Lis Loaf, page 94. *Top:* Lotus Blossom T-shirt, page 51. *Bottom:* Monogrammed Tote, page 47. *Opposite:* Olive-Branch Summer Dress, page 43.

Top: Victorian Satin Sheets and Pillowcases, page 58.
Above: Water Lily Treasure Box, page 153.

Well-Dressed Turkey

To our way of thinking, every major dinner-guest list should include, as guest of honor, Count Wellington, the best-dressed turkey in town. He'll not only charm your guests and warm their hearts and tummies, he'll make your meal a feast straight from the pages of a Charles Dickens novel. Naturally, you can adapt our wardrobe design to fit a smaller fowl, such as a chicken or Cornish hen.

Materials:
1 turkey, 18 pounds
Butter Pastry (recipe follows)
waxed paper
string *or* **twine**
1 piece illustration board, 15 by 20 inches
scissors
1 sheet stencil paper, 18 by 24 inches
masking tape
#1 X-acto knife with #11 blades
1 egg yolk
muffin tin
food coloring, in red, blue, and green
1 watercolor brush, #5
sharp kitchen knife

Procedure:

1. We always use this delicious butter pastry to dress the turkey because it looks and tastes so good; however, you can also use a pie-crust mix if you wish. If you are using our recipe, remember that this pastry softens easily. If it becomes too soft to work with, place it in the refrigerator for a few minutes.

Butter Pastry

3 cups all-purpose flour	1 teaspoon salt
½ pound (2 sticks) butter, chilled	½ cup plus 2 tablespoons ice water
⅓ cup vegetable shortening	

Place the flour in a large mixing bowl. Cut the chilled butter into small bits; using a pastry blender, blend the butter along with the shortening into the flour until the mixture resembles coarse meal. Do not overwork the dough, as the butter should not be allowed to soften. Add the salt and ice water (ice water can be made by shaking water and ice cubes together in a covered jar before measuring); mix rapidly until the two are well blended and form a stiff dough. Shape the dough into a flat round, wrap it in waxed paper, and chill it for at least 3 hours or overnight.

2. Use your favorite family recipe for roast turkey, stuffed or unstuffed, making sure that you tie the legs together with string or twine and bend the wing tips underneath the turkey. Brush the turkey with melted butter before roasting and several times during the roasting. Roast the turkey as you usually would, but remove it from the oven 15 minutes before the cooking is complete.

3. While the turkey is roasting and the pastry chilling, prepare the stencils for the turkey's "dressing." Enlarge each of the four designs to size on the illustration board (see page 14), allowing at least 2 inches of space between the designs. Trim the stencil paper so that it is slightly smaller than the illustration board and tape it in place over the designs. Cut out the stencil openings with the X-acto knife; then cut out the vest shape along the dotted lines.

4. When the pastry is thoroughly chilled, roll it out on a lightly floured

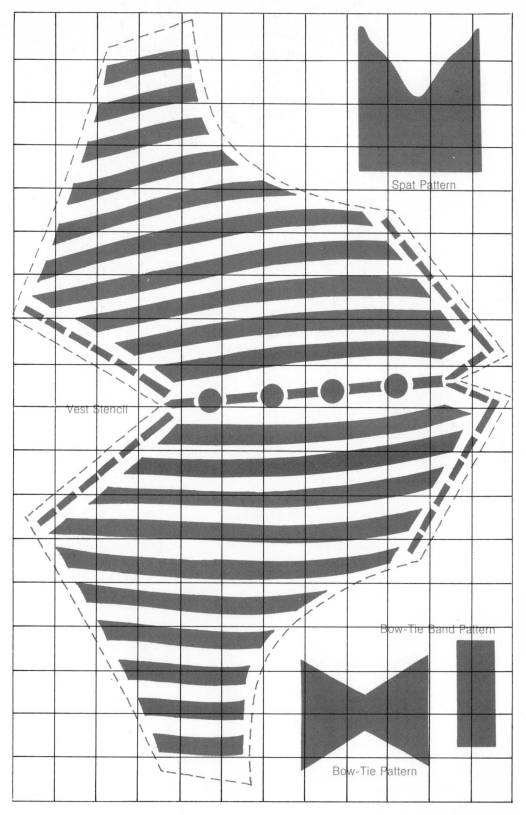

Spat Pattern

Vest Stencil

Bow-Tie Band Pattern

Bow-Tie Pattern

Each square = 1 inch

surface to a ⅛-inch thickness. Cut it into a rectangle that measures 12 by 17 inches, and place it on a sheet of waxed paper that is slightly larger than the dough; reserve the dough scraps for another project. Center the vest stencil over the pastry. Run your fingers lightly over the stencil, gently pressing the stencil to the pastry; the moisture in the pastry will hold the stencil in place.

5.   For this project, you will need a base mixture of egg yolk and water to which food coloring is added. To make this base, place an egg yolk and a teaspoon of water in a cup and mix them thoroughly. Place 1 teaspoon of the yolk base into one well of the muffin tin; add enough red food coloring to make a bright red food paint; the amount of color you add depends on the shade you want. Place ½ teaspoon of the plain yolk base in each of two wells of the muffin tin; add several drops of green food coloring to one section to make a bright green food paint, and, to the other section, add 2 drops of red food coloring, 2 drops of blue food coloring, and 2 drops of green food coloring to make a black food paint. Reserve the remaining plain yolk base to attach the bow tie later.

6.   Dip the tip of the brush into the red food paint and remove the excess by gently pressing the bristles against the side of the muffin-tin well. Being careful not to rest your hands on the pastry as you work, begin stenciling the stripes of the vest by filling in each stencil opening with an even coat of red food paint. Make sure that you do not have too much color on your brush; if you do, it may run under the edges of the stencil openings and result in a messy design. Do not go back over your design too many times —overworking food paint on unbaked dough may result in scruffy designs. When you have finished painting the stripes, rinse the brush in water and then dip it into the green food paint. Using the same stenciling procedure, stencil the stitched design around the vest. Rinse out the brush again, and stencil the button shapes with the black food paint.

7.   Lay the pattern pieces for the bow tie (the bow-tie shape and the rectangular band shape) and the spat on the unstenciled areas of the dough surrounding the vest. Cut around the shapes with a sharp knife, using the outside edges of the pattern pieces as a cutting guide. Reposition the spat pattern and cut a second spat. Pick up all the scraps of dough and save them for another use. Using the black food paint and the brush, make four button shapes on each spat; the buttons of one spat should be on the right-hand side and the buttons on the other should be on the left. Refrigerate all the stenciled and cutout pastry shapes until they are firm.

8.   When the turkey is 15 minutes away from being done, remove it from the oven and increase the oven temperature to 425° F. While the oven is heating, arrange the pastry clothes on the turkey. Unless your hands are very large, you may need some help in placing the pastry vest on the turkey. To do it, carefully lift the vest from the waxed paper, spreading your fingers as far apart as possible, and arrange it over the turkey. If the sleeve sections are a little too long for your turkey, simply cut away the excess dough with kitchen shears or a knife. Wrap the rectangular band section of the bow tie around the bow-tie shape, as shown.

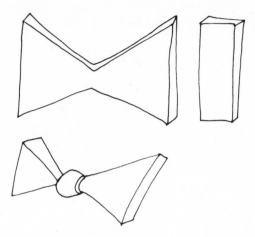

Brush the reserved plain yolk base over the bottom of the bow tie and center it over the top of the V of the vest neckline. Add the spats by gently wrapping each of them over a drumstick, as shown.

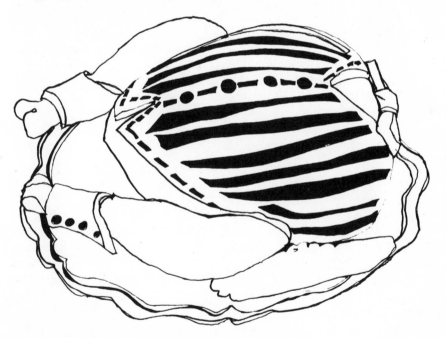

They do not need the yolk base to hold them in place.

9. Bake the "dressed" turkey for about 15 minutes, or until the pastry is crisp and the edges are golden brown. Remove the turkey from the oven and let it rest for from 15 to 20 minutes before carving.

Hints and Ideas:

★If any of your stenciled designs should crack before or during baking, touch up the crack with food paint and the brush.

★For well-dressed chickens or smaller turkeys, scale this design down and then follow the same procedure.

Picture-Perfect Pie and Box

Once you learn the relatively simple art of picture-pie making, you'll never be at a loss for an unusual gift. You can make picture pies, portrait pies, and pretty pies with poppies, petunias, and pansies. You'll always be able to delight and amaze your host or hostess with a beautifully painted pie in a box with a matching top.

Materials:

Cherry Pie Filling (recipe follows)
1 box (10 ounces) pie-crust mix
waxed paper
1 piece illustration board, 15 by 20 inches
masking tape
1 sheet stencil paper, 18 by 24 inches
#1 X-acto knife with #11 blades
1 egg yolk
muffin tin
set of food coloring, containing red, yellow, blue, and green
1 watercolor brush, #5
1 plain white box, 10 by 10 by 2 inches
newspaper
1 can spray paint, in blue

Procedure:

1.   Prepare the cherry pie filling, using our recipe or one of your own if you wish. If you are using one of your own, choose one that won't bubble over while baking and ruin the stenciled design.

Grandma Betts's Cherry Pie Filling

⅓ cup all-purpose flour	3 tablespoons honey
¾ cup sugar	¼ teaspoon grated lemon rind
¼ teaspoon salt	¼ cup (½ stick) butter
2 cans (1 pound each) tart red pitted cherries, in water	½ teaspoon almond extract
	3 drops red food coloring (optional)
¾ cup cherry juice (drained from cherries)	

Blend the flour, sugar, and salt together in a small bowl; set the mixture aside. Drain the cherries and set them aside; reserve ¾ cup of the cherry liquid. Place the cherry liquid in a medium saucepan along with the honey; stir in the flour mixture. Cook over medium heat, stirring constantly, until the mixture thickens and begins to boil; reduce the heat and simmer, stirring, for 3 minutes. Remove the mixture from the heat and stir in the reserved cherries, lemon rind, butter, almond extract, and food coloring. Cover the mixture with a round of waxed paper and refrigerate it until cooled.

2.   Prepare the pastry for a two-crust pie, following the directions on the package. Divide the pastry into two parts, one slightly larger than the other. Roll out the smaller part to form an 11-inch circle; refrigerate the larger part until needed. Place the pastry circle on a piece of waxed paper slightly larger than the dough; cover it with waxed paper and refrigerate it until needed.

3.   Enlarge the stencil design to size on the illustration board (see page 14). Trim the stencil paper slightly smaller than the illustration board, and tape it in place over the design. Using the X-acto knife, cut out the design and then cut around the design, leaving at least a 1-inch margin all around.

4.   For this project, you will need a base mixture of egg yolk and water to which the food coloring is added. To make this base, place one egg yolk and one teaspoon of water in a cup and mix thoroughly. Place ½ teaspoon

Each square = 1 inch

of the yolk base into each of four wells of the muffin tin, and add several drops of food coloring to each to make red, blue, yellow, and green food paint. The amount of color you add depends on the shade you want. Set aside the remaining yolk base.

5.   Place the stencil in the center of the 11-inch pastry circle, and run your fingers lightly over the stencil to press it into the pastry. The moisture in the pastry will hold it in place. Take care that you do not rest your hands on the pastry as you stencil. If the pastry becomes soft as you are stenciling it, return it to the refrigerator for a few minutes to chill; then remove it and resume stenciling.

6.   Dip the tip of the watercolor brush into the red food paint, and remove the excess color from the brush by pressing the bristles lightly against the side of the muffin-tin well. Stencil the center medallion shape with an even coat of red. Make sure that you do not have too much color on your brush or it will run under the edges of the stencil openings and result in a messy design. For best results, do not go back over your design too many times;

overworking food coloring on unbaked pastry will also result in a messy design.

7.   Following the color key given in the illustration, stencil the remainder of the design.

Blue

Green

Yellow

Red

Make sure that you rinse the brush out in clean water before dipping it into the next color. Carefully remove the stencil when you have completed the design, and refrigerate the stenciled pastry until it is firm. Do not delay completion of the pie for a prolonged time, however, for the pastry will dry out.

8.   Preheat the oven to 425° F. Roll out the reserved pastry into a 13-inch circle and fit it loosely into a 9-inch pie plate. Do not stretch the pastry. Pour the cooled cherry pie filling into the shell. Moisten the edges of the pie shell with water. Carefully remove the stenciled pastry from the waxed paper and center it over the filling. Crimp the edges together and fold the overhang under. Make a decorative fluting all around and brush the fluting with the remaining uncolored egg-yolk base. Cut four ½-inch slits in the center medallion. Bake the pie for 35 minutes, or until it is lightly browned and the pastry is done. Serves 6 to 8.

9.   After you have finished making the pie, use the stencil to decorate a box that will turn your pie into a one-of-a-kind gift. First, you need to extend the edges of the stencil to prevent the spray paint from getting on the box

where it shouldn't. Do this by cutting out an 8-inch square from the center of a large sheet of paper, such as newspaper. Place the paper over the stencil and tape it into place, as shown.

Center the extended stencil over the top of the box, making sure that the stencil lies as close to the surface of the box as possible. Place a layer of newspaper under the box, and, holding the spray paint about 20 inches away from the box, lightly spray downward. If you hold the can of spray paint too close to the box or use it with too much force, the stencil may lift up or shift and create a messy design. After all the stencil openings have been coated with a thin layer of paint, let the design dry and remove the stencil.

Hints and Ideas:

★If you can't find a box that's 10 inches square, ask your bakery for a plain pie box and use that.

★If any of the stencil designs on the pie crack before or during baking, touch them up with food color or food paint and a brush.

★After you have stenciled the box, do not use that stencil again on food—cut a new one instead.

Message Cookies

Message cookies add an element of fun to gift-giving and party menus. With this recipe for delicious cream-cheese shortbread cookies, a set of modular ABC stencils, and a box of food colors, you can make every bite a personal one.

Instead of sending an ordinary card to someone you love, stencil an affectionate message on a batch of cookies. Or, for dessert at your next dinner party, serve each guest two cookies stenciled with his or her own initials. Message Cookies are perfect for children's parties: Use them for place cards, slogans, or for an edible word game. However you use them, Message Cookies will make you happy to eat your own words.

Materials:

Cream-Cheese Shortbread Cookie Dough (recipe follows)
1 piece illustration board, 15 by 20 inches
scissors
1 sheet stencil paper, 18 by 24 inches
masking tape
#1 X-acto knife with #11 blades
muffin tin
set of food coloring, containing red, yellow, blue, and green
waxed paper
1 watercolor brush, #5

Procedure:

1. Prepare the cookie dough, following the recipe given below.

Cream-Cheese Shortbread Cookie Dough

½ pound (2 sticks) butter	dash of salt
1 package (8 ounces) cream cheese	¾ cup sugar
3½ cups all-purpose flour	

Let the butter and cream cheese soften to room temperature (about 30 minutes). In a large bowl, mash the butter with a wooden spoon and mix in the flour and salt; blend well, using your hands if you wish. Add the softened cream cheese and the sugar to the flour mixture and mix them well to form a stiff dough. Using a rolling pin, roll out the dough to a ¼ -inch thickness on a lightly floured surface. Cut the cookies into rectangles that measured 2 by 2¾ inches.

2. After you have decided upon what message or name you would like to spell out with your cookies, enlarge to size each of the necessary letters on the illustration board (see page 14). Cut the stencil paper into sections that are about an inch larger all around than one of the enlarged letters. Tape one section over each letter, and cut the stencil with the X-acto knife.

3. Determine how many different colors you'd like to make your letters; then, for each color you wish to use, place ½ teaspoon water in a well of the muffin tin. Add several drops of food color to each well. The amount of color you add depends on the shade you want—it's a good idea to test the colors on a small piece of cookie dough before you begin stenciling with them. To make orange food color, add a bit of red to some yellow; to make brown, add a tiny bit of blue to the orange.

4. Lay one unbaked cookie on a small piece of waxed paper and center one of the letter stencils on top. (Trim any cookie that is to be stenciled with the letter "I" to a 1-inch width.) Dip the tip of the brush into the color you wish and remove the excess by gently pressing the bristles against the side of the well. Holding the stencil in place with your hand, trace through the stencil opening with the tip of the brush. Continue to apply color until the exposed area is evenly coated. Avoid going back over the design too many times, for overworking food color on unbaked dough may result in a messy design. Place the stenciled cookie on an ungreased cookie sheet.

5. Lay another cookie on the waxed paper and stencil it with another letter, using the same stenciling procedure described in step 4. Continue

stenciling in this manner until all the cookies have been painted. Be sure to rinse out your brush each time that you change colors. As you place the completed cookies on the cookie sheet, leave about ½ inch of space between cookies. When all the cookies have been stenciled or when the cookie sheet is full, place them in an oven preheated to 350° F. Bake them for about 15 minutes, or until they are slightly browned. Cool the cookies for 5 minutes on the cookie sheet and then remove them to brown wrapping paper to cool completely.

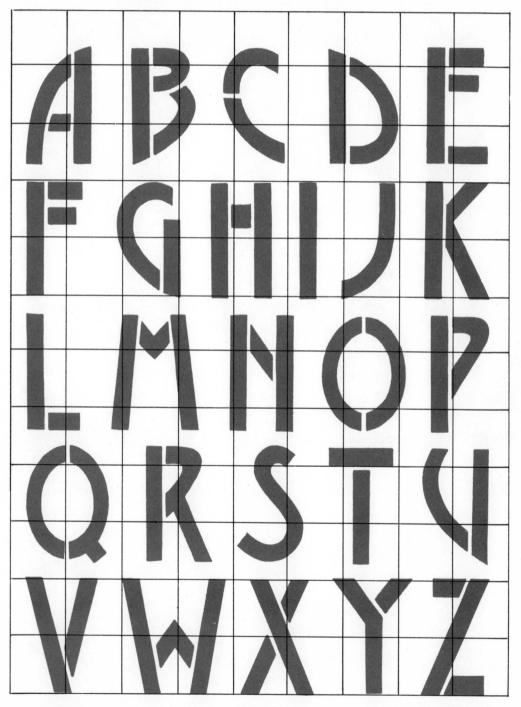

Each square = 1 inch

Sugar-Sifted Brownies

Remember the trick of placing a paper doily over a cake and then sifting powdered sugar through it to create a lacy, snowflake pattern? Doilies are nice, but with stencils, you can create a design to fit every occasion and make every individual portion carry a complete design.

Besides powdered sugar, there are many other decorative food products that can be applied through stencils to brighten up your table. For brilliant stained-glass effects, carefully sift colored sugar sparkles and candy confetti through stencils. Or, try using a stencil as a guide to stud a festive cake top with chocolate chips, silver dragées, and bits of red and green maraschino cherries.

Materials:
Rich Chocolate Brownies (recipe follows)
1 piece illustration board, 6 inches square
masking tape
1 piece stencil paper, 5 inches square
#1 X-acto knife with #11 blades
mesh strainer *or* sifter
confectioners sugar (about 1 cup)

Procedure:

1.   Prepare the recipe for brownies that follows, or use one of your own if you wish. This recipe, however, is exceptionally rich and produces the perfect deep shade of brown to show off snow white powdered sugar designs.

Rich Chocolate Brownies

5 squares (1 ounce each) unsweetened chocolate	2 cups sugar
	1 tablespoon vanilla extract
¼ pound (1 stick) butter	1 cup all-purpose flour
½ cup vegetable shortening	½ teaspoon baking soda
4 eggs	1 cup chopped walnuts
¼ teaspoon salt	

Preheat the oven to 325° F. Generously grease a 9-inch-square baking pan. Place the chocolate, butter, and shortening in a small saucepan and place it over very low heat; stir occasionally until the mixture is thoroughly melted. Remove the mixture from the heat and let it cool slightly—do not refrigerate it. Beat the eggs and salt together in a large mixing bowl until they are well blended; gradually add the sugar and continue beating until the mixture is creamy. Add the chocolate mixture and the vanilla; fold in well. Add the flour, baking soda, and walnuts all at once and beat only until the mixture is well blended. Pour it into the greased pan and bake it 45 to 50 minutes, or until a toothpick inserted in the center comes out clean. Cool 5 minutes and cut into 3-inch squares.

2.   While the brownies are baking, transfer the stencil design onto the illustration board (see page 15) and tape the stencil paper in place over the design. Using the X-acto knife, cut the stencil and then cut around it, leaving a 1-inch border all around.

3.   For best results, the brownies should still be warm while they are being stenciled. Turn the brownies upside down so that you can do the stenciling on the bottom side instead of the top—the bottom side is smoother and therefore a better stenciling surface. Place one brownie on a large plate—to catch the extra confectioners sugar—and center the stencil on top of the brownie.

4.   Holding the strainer or sifter in one hand directly over the stencil-covered brownie and a small amount of confectioners sugar in the other, slowly sprinkle the sugar down through the sifter while you are quickly moving the sifter back and forth across the stencil. Hold the sifter about 1 inch above the top of the brownie, and continue sifting until all the stencil openings have been *lightly* coated with confectioners sugar—too much confectioners sugar will result in a messy design.

5.   When the stencil openings have been lightly and evenly coated with the confectioners sugar, *carefully* lift the stencil up. Make sure that you are lifting the stencil straight up and not at an angle. Move the stencil to an empty plate and shake off the sugar that has accumulated on the stencil.

6.   Place the stencil on top of another brownie and sift the sugar over it. Repeat this procedure until all the brownies have been stenciled. Serve the brownies with whipped cream and maraschino cherries if desired.

Celebration Cake

Several years ago, we met a Greek man who was a master of the craft of decorating cakes. His studio—since he is as much sculptor as baker, no other word is appropriate—was located in a once-fashionable area that is now a slum. In better times, he had busily fashioned his masterpieces for the carriage trade. But times had changed; his doors were closed, and it was very rare that the full use of his talents was called upon.

His studio was lined with dusty showcases that housed examples of his art; among them were spun-sugar baskets, actually woven, that contained crystalline bouquets of wildflowers and long-stemmed roses that seemed to be made of fine Venetian glass. It was sad in a way to listen to this fine old gentleman talk of past glories; he had become an anachronism in an age in which things are stamped out by the thousands.

This project is designed to celebrate the artist lurking in all of us. Time does indeed march on; this cake is to help make even more extraordinary those warm, special occasions that celebrate milestones along the way.

Materials:

1 piece illustration board, 15 by 20 inches
scissors
1 sheet stencil paper, 18 by 24 inches
masking tape
#1 X-acto knife with #11 blades
Cream-Cheese Shortbread Cookie Dough (recipe on page 116)
muffin tin
set of food coloring, containing red, yellow, blue, and green
2 watercolor brushes, one #5 and one #3
Uncle Jim's Carrot Cake (recipe follows)
Cream Cheese Frosting (recipe follows)

Procedure:

1.   Transfer the stencil design to the illustration board (see page 15), trim the stencil paper so that it is slightly smaller than the illustration board, and tape it in place over the design. Using the X-acto knife, cut the stencil carefully—there are many delicate bridges (see page 19 for stencil repair). Then cut around the stencil design, allowing at least a 1-inch border all around.

2.   Prepare the cookie dough, roll it out on a lightly floured surface to a ¼-inch thickness, and cut it into a 7½- by 10½-inch rectangle. Lift the cookie-dough rectangle onto an ungreased cookie sheet, and center the stencil on top of the dough. Lightly run your fingers across the stencil, gently pressing it into the surface of the dough; the moisture of the dough will hold the stencil in place.

3.   Place ½ teaspoon of water into each of six muffin-tin wells and add several drops of food coloring to each to make the following colors: yellow, yellow green (2 drops yellow, 1 green), green, light blue (less color), red, and light red (less color). The amount of color you add depends on the shades you want.

4.   The rule to remember while you are painting this design is to start with the lighter colors and build up to the darker ones. Dip the tip of the #5 brush in the light red food color and remove the excess color from the brush by gently pressing the bristles against the side of the muffin-tin well. Make sure that the brush is relatively dry; excess color on the brush will run under the edges of the stencil and result in a messy design. Lightly paint all the petal shapes with the light red. You needn't try to obtain an even coating of color as you paint through the stencil openings; obvious brush strokes will enhance the final design and give it a "painterly" effect. When all the petal shapes have been filled in, wash the brush with water, dip it into the darker red, and repaint some of the petals a darker red. Wash the brush again, dip it into the yellow, and highlight some of the petal shapes. Wash the brush.

5.   Dip the clean #5 brush into the yellow green and paint all the leaves. Then wash the brush, dip it into the green, and repaint most of the leaves green; let some of the yellow green show through. Dip the #3 brush into the green and paint the stems. Wash both brushes.

6.   Using the clean #5 brush, paint the square light blue. Outline the square with the #3 brush and the green food color. Using the same brush and any color, write an appropriate message inside the square. Remove the stencil and bake the cookie top according to the directions. Empty the color from the muffin tin and wash the brushes.

7.   After the cookie top has been baked, remove it from the oven and place the cookie sheet—with the cookie top still on it—in the refrigerator or freezer to chill thoroughly. In the meantime, prepare and frost the cake.

Uncle Jim's Carrot Cake

2½ cups all-purpose flour
  1 teaspoon baking powder
  1 teaspoon baking soda
  1 teaspoon salt
  2 teaspoons ground cinnamon
1½ cups vegetable oil

  2 cups sugar
  5 eggs
  3 cups shredded carrots, firmly packed
1½ cups chopped walnuts
Cream Cheese Frosting (recipe follows)

Preheat the oven to 350° F. Grease and lightly flour a 13 × 9 × 2-inch baking pan; set it aside. In a medium bowl, sift together the flour, baking powder, baking soda, salt, and cinnamon; set it aside. In a large bowl, combine the oil and sugar and mix them thoroughly. Add one egg at a time, beating well after each addition. Add the flour mixture, one-third at a time, stirring well after each addition; beat until the mixture is smooth. Add the carrots and walnuts and stir until they are evenly distributed. Pour the mixture into the prepared pan and bake in a preheated oven for 50 to 60 minutes, or until a toothpick inserted in the center comes out clean. Cool in the pan for 15 minutes. Run a knife around the edge of the cake to loosen it from the pan, and invert the cake onto the platter or board that it is to be served on. When the cake is completely cooled, frost it with Cream Cheese Frosting.

Cream Cheese Frosting

  1 package (8 ounces) cream cheese
¼ cup (½ stick) butter

  1 box (1 pound) confectioners sugar

Let the cream cheese and butter soften to room temperature (about 30 minutes). Place the cream cheese and butter in a medium bowl and beat until fluffy. Gradually stir in the sugar. Do not refrigerate the frosting before decorating the cake or it will set. Frost the sides of the cake first and then the top.

8.   Remove the stenciled cookie top from the refrigerator and position it on top of the frosted cake. If the cookie top sticks to the cookie sheet, place the cookie sheet over a lighted stove burner for 2 or 3 seconds; the heat will loosen the cookie top. Pipe a decorative border around the cookie top and around the base of the cake by squeezing the remaining frosting through a pastry bag. Refrigerate the cake until one hour before serving time.

Note: This carrot cake tastes best the second or third day after making.

Hints and Ideas:

★If you need to save time, buy a cake from the bakery instead of making one and use canned frosting.

★The cookie top alone—stenciled, of course—makes a great gift.

Garden Party Sandwiches

Even though the sandwich was invented by a European, the Earl of Sandwich, it's in the United States that the sandwich is most at home. It is called by hundreds of names and served in hundreds of ways—hot and cold, large and small, simple and complicated.

One of our specialties used to be the giant hamburger: a large, round loaf of bread split to house a giant meat patty and then sliced into wedges like a pie. When this monster was served along with giant French fries, family-sized bottles of catsup, thick slices of beefsteak tomatoes, and king-sized malts, the table looked as though it had been prepared for Paul Bunyan.

This project is an easy exercise in sprucing up any sandwich, quickly and easily. These perky party sandwiches are great for bridge parties, intimate late-night suppers, and, as their name implies, garden parties.

Materials:
2 slices white bread (only one slice will be stenciled)
1 piece illustration board, 5 by 7 inches
masking tape
1 piece stencil paper, 4 by 6 inches
#1 X-acto knife with #11 blades
food coloring, in red and green
1 watercolor brush, #5
"Our Hero" sandwich (recipe follows)

Procedure:

1. Transfer the stencil design to the illustration board (see page 15),

and tape the stencil paper in place over the design. Cut the stencil with the X-acto knife. Position the cut stencil on top of one slice of bread, as shown.

2. Place ½ teaspoon of water in each of two cups. Add several drops of the red food coloring to one and several drops of green to the other—the amount of food coloring you add depends on the shade you want. Dip the tip of the brush into the red food coloring. Holding the stencil in place with one hand and the brush with the other, apply the color through only the flower openings of the stencil. Since the bread will rapidly absorb the

color, you needn't worry about the color running under the stencil and ruining the design. Wash the brush when you have completed the flower and dip it into the green; stencil the leaves.

3. Lift up the stencil, turn it around, and reposition it on the bread, as shown.

Using the same procedures described in step 2, stencil the design again.

4. Lightly toast both slices of bread (one stenciled, one unstenciled) until only the edges are toasted. Prepare the sandwich, following the recipe given below, and then cut it diagonally so that each part of the sandwich contains a complete design. Serve it with carrot curls and potato chips.

"Our Hero"

2 slices lightly toasted white bread (one stenciled)	1 slice salami
1 tablespoon mayonnaise	2 slices olive-pimiento loaf
½ teaspoon prepared mustard	2 slices American cheese
	lettuce leaves

Place the unstenciled slice of bread on a plate. Mix the mayonnaise and the mustard together in a small cup until well blended; spread the mixture evenly over the bread on the plate. Arrange the meats, cheese, and lettuce over the mayonnaise mixture and top it with the stenciled slice of bread, making sure that the stenciled side is up.

Hints and Ideas:

★Try other sandwich fillings in your stenciled sandwiches.

★For a unique party or luncheon, stencil placemats and napkins to match the sandwiches.

Fiesta Chili Pie

Below the festive crust of this main-dish pie lies a hearty filling with a South-of-the-Border flavor. Our love for Mexican food developed during our California days, when we used to mix chili powder with water to paint Aztec designs on tortillas that were then baked on top of various tasty *cazuelas* (casseroles).

If Mexican food is a bit too spicy for your palate, translate this concept into a dish of your own choosing: a chicken pot pie with a stenciled chicken on top or a beef stew pie with a garland of stenciled fresh vegetables bordering the edges.

Materials:

Chili con Carne (recipe follows)
1 box (10 ounces) pie-crust mix
waxed paper
1 piece illustration board, 15 by 20 inches
scissors
1 sheet stencil paper, 18 by 24 inches
masking tape
#1 X-acto knife with #11 blades
1 egg yolk
muffin tin
set of food coloring, containing red, yellow, blue, and green
1 watercolor brush, #5

Procedure:

1.   Prepare the chili before you begin stenciling, using the following recipe or one of your own.

Chili con Carne

2 pounds ground chuck	2 to 3 tablespoons chili powder
2 cups chopped onion	1 can (1 pound, 12 ounces) tomatoes
2 garlic cloves, finely minced	1 can (8 ounces) tomato sauce
2 cups finely diced green pepper	2 cups water
2 teaspoons ground cumin *(cominos)*	2 cans (1 pound each) pinto beans *or*
1 tablespoon whole fennel seed	red kidney beans, drained
2 teaspoons salt	3 tablespoons yellow cornmeal
⅛ teaspoon pepper	2 cups cheddar cheese, shredded

Brown the meat in a large skillet, breaking it up with a wooden spoon as it browns. Drain off all but 2 tablespoons of the fat and transfer the contents of the skillet to a large kettle or Dutch oven. Add the onion, garlic, and green pepper to the mixture. Cook over medium heat about 5 minutes, stirring occasionally. Stir in the cumin, fennel seed, salt, pepper, and chili powder. Chop the tomatoes roughly and add them (with the juice) to the mixture along with the tomato sauce and water. Bring the mixture to a boil, reduce the heat, and simmer, uncovered, for 45 minutes. Add the beans and simmer over low heat for about 30 minutes, stirring occasionally. Blend in the cornmeal and cook 3 minutes longer. You will use the cheese in step 8, when you assemble the casserole.

2.   While the chili is simmering, prepare the pie crust according to the package instructions and roll it out on a lightly floured board to form a rectangle measuring 11 by 15 inches. Place it on a square of waxed paper that is slightly larger than the dough. Cover it with waxed paper and refrigerate it until needed. Do not delay the completion of the pie for a prolonged time or the pastry will dry out.

3.   Enlarge the design to size on the illustration board (see page 14). Trim the stencil paper so that it is slightly smaller than the illustration board and tape it in place over the design. Using the X-acto knife, cut the stencil. Then cut around the stencil, leaving a 1-inch border all around.

4.   To stencil this project, you will need a base mixture of egg yolk and water to which food coloring is added. To make this base, place an egg yolk and 1 teaspoon water in a cup and mix thoroughly. Then place ½

Each square = 1 inch

teaspoon of the yolk base into each of six wells of a muffin tin and add several drops of food coloring to each to make the following colors: red, light red (less color), orange (red and yellow mixed), blue, green, and black (2 drops each of red, blue, and green). The amount of color you add depends on the shade you want. Reserve the remaining base.

5.   Remove the pastry from the refrigerator and center the stencil on top. Run your fingers lightly over the stencil, gently pressing the stencil to the pastry; the moisture in the pastry will hold the stencil in place. Take care that you do not rest your hands on the pastry as you stencil. If the pastry gets soft as you stencil, chill it for a few minutes, leaving the stencil in place, and then resume stenciling.

6.   Dip the tip of the watercolor brush into the orange food paint and remove the excess color from the brush by gently pressing the bristles on the side of the muffin-tin well. Starting with the word *Olé!,* begin stenciling by filling in each letter with an even coat of food paint. Make sure that you do not have too much color on your brush or it will run under the edges of the stencil openings. Do not go back over your design with the food paint too many times; if you do, the finished design will not be crisp. Rinse out your brush.

7.   Dip the brush into the red food paint and color in every other—alternating—chevron shape in the border around *Olé!* Fill in the remaining chevron shapes with the black food paint. (Be sure that you wash the brush first before using the black.) Use the same black to outline each of the letters in the word *Olé!* and to make a small dot in the center of the "O." Paint the polka dots with light red (pink) and green, alternating the colors as you stencil. Use red food paint to stencil the wavy border line. Complete the stenciling of the pie by alternating all the colors in your muffin-tin wells around the outside border. Carefully remove the stencil and chill the pastry until firm.

8.   Preheat the oven to 425° F. Place half the chili filling—it should be hot —into a 13 × 9 × 2-inch baking pan and sprinkle it evenly with the cheese. Top it with the remaining chili, spreading it evenly. Carefully lift the stenciled pastry from the waxed paper and center it over the filling in the pan. Turn the edges under all around and make a decorative fluting; brush the fluting with the leftover plain yolk base. Cut four ½-inch slits in the pastry around the world *Olé!* Bake for 25 minutes, or until the edges are lightly browned. Serves 10.

Hints and Ideas:

★If any of the stenciled designs crack before or during baking, touch them up with food paint and a brush.

4
Wood

Prepare unfinished wood by sanding with fine sandpaper. (For floors, rent a commercial sander.) Remove sanding dust; wipe away any remaining traces with a damp sponge. If desired, apply wood stain at this point. Stencil with acrylics, latex paints, spray paints, japan colors, or marking pens. Beautiful parquet effects can be obtained on unfinished wood by stenciling with different shades of wood stains. Apply wood stains with cheesecloth, a sponge, or a cotton ball; whichever you use, be sure to squeeze the applicator almost dry before applying. Wipe away any excess stain immediately. Protect designs on unfinished woods with clear polyurethane, varnish, or other transparent coating. (If

you stenciled with marking pens, test the coating before applying; some coatings dissolve inks.) Wicker and similar surfaces can be stenciled on with acrylics; because of the uneven surface, designs should be kept simple. In most cases, wood paneling can be stenciled with acrylics; if your paneling is very slick or shiny, use japan colors or enamels. When stenciling finished woods, be sure that the surface is clean and dry. No protective coating is required on finished woods unless otherwise noted. *Acrylics:* Stencil over acrylic-painted wood with either acrylic paints or latex enamels. *Deck paints:* Stencil over woods painted with deck paints with additional deck paints in a contrasting color. Keep in mind that deck paints require a long drying time. *Flat*

latex paints: Stencil over woods painted with flat latex paints with acrylics, latex paints, permanent marking pens, spray paints, japan colors, or sizing for gold leaf. *Latex enamels:* Stencil over woods painted with latex enamels with acrylics, latex enamels, deck paints, spray enamels, or sizing for gold leaf. *Varnish, shellac:* If the surface is very glossy, stencil with japan colors or enamels. Or, knock down the gloss slightly with wet, fine sandpaper or fine steel wool and then stencil with acrylics or enamels. A third possibility is to remove the finish with liquid paint and varnish remover or sandpaper and then stencil as you would unfinished wood.

Decorative Chopping Block

As a youngster, Jim F. spent a summer—summers seemed so long then—with his cousins and aunt and uncle on a small farm in the Midwest. In town was a library, and in the library was a librarian who was very fond of the tales of King Arthur. It wasn't long before the farm became Camelot.

The hayloft was the dank castle of the wicked Morgan le Fay. After besieging the loft, they would venture into the fields to do battle with the scarecrows and cornstalks. They even spent time by the side of the pond, waiting for the Lady of the Lake to emerge with a silver chalice. Cows became dragons, pigs became boars, and they became exhausted.

At dusk, a weary, dusty crew would trudge back to the farmhouse. After cleanup and inspection, the daytime knights would spend the rest of the evening around the kitchen table, playing games while Aunt Charlotte canned, pickled, and preserved. Something good was always bubbling on top of the big cast-iron stove, and the group at the table happily gobbled all the goodies they were offered.

Jim often wishes he were back in that old-fashioned country kitchen, watching his aunt slicing fresh-baked bread on a worn butcher block and then serving it with homemade butter and jam. For a treat like that, he'd gladly fight a scarecrow.

Materials:

chopping block, 12 by 12 inches
1 piece illustration board, 15 by 20 inches
masking tape
1 sheet stencil paper, 18 by 24 inches
#1 X-acto knife with #11 blades
acrylic tube paints, in red, blue, yellow, pink, and green
paper plates
5 stencil brushes, all #1*
newspaper

*Very small stencil brushes must be used for this project so that the colors are stenciled only in the areas for which they were intended.

Procedure:

1. Enlarge both stencil designs to size on the illustration board (see page 14), allowing at least 2 inches of space between the designs. Trim the stencil paper slightly smaller than the illustration board and tape it in place over the designs. Using the X-acto knife, cut out the inner designs and then cut out around the stencils, allowing a 1-inch margin all around.

Border Stencil

Design Stencil

Each square = 1 inch

2. Complete the stenciling of the border first—the border design will be repeated four times. Place the border stencil in one corner of the board and tape it into place. Squeeze a small amount of red paint onto one

paper plate, blue onto another, and yellow onto another. Using three different stencil brushes, stencil the outer row of chevrons with red, the middle row of diamonds with blue, and the inner row of chevrons with yellow. Apply the paint with an up-and-down dabbing motion, and make sure that the brush you are using is fairly dry—remove any excess paint by pouncing the brush on some newspaper. When all the openings have been evenly coated with the appropriate colors, lift the stencil straight up and reposition it in the next corner. Using exactly the same techniques described earlier, stencil this portion of the border. Reposition and stencil the design in the remaining two corners to complete the border. Allow the paint to dry.

3.   Center the design stencil within the stenciled border and tape it to the board in several places. Beginning with the blue paint and following the illustration below labeled blue, fill in the areas shown as solid black. Using the yellow paint and following the illustration labeled yellow, fill in the black areas. Add the pink and green elements to the design in the same way.

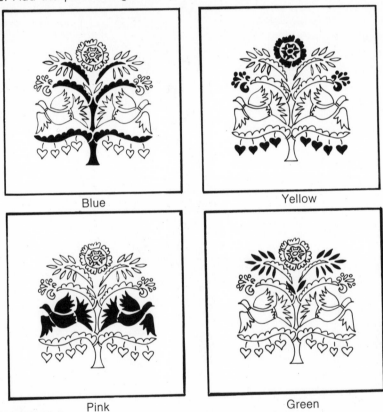

Blue

Yellow

Pink

Green

Hints and Ideas:

★Some red paints are very transparent. If you find yours too transparent, stencil the design with two coats of paint, leaving the stencil in place and allowing the paint to dry between coats.

★Try stenciling this design with acrylic paints on fabric and then embroidering over the design.

★Do not chop food on the painted side of the chopping block. Use the unpainted side for that chore.

Sporty Spare Chair

Almost everyone has a piece of furniture that could use a little revamping. An old, secondhand chest-of-drawers, perhaps, with missing knobs and chipping paint or a nightstand that was once fashionable but has long since lost its aesthetic charm. (Remember the "blond" furniture from the forties and fifties?) Even new furniture doesn't always make the statement you'd like it to make.

The obvious solution to these decorating dilemmas is stenciling. With a lovely stenciled design, you can turn any unattractive piece of furniture into a one-of-a-kind, handcrafted treasure.

We bought an inexpensive wooden folding chair for this project. Painted in flat white, it's handsomely designed and has clean, simple lines. We accentuated the contemporary lines of the chair by designing a rather modern border that frames the chair's structure.

Materials:

wooden folding chair with a slatted seat and a flat white finish*
1 piece illustration board, 20 by 30 inches
masking tape
2 sheets stencil paper, each 18 by 24 inches
#1 X-acto knife with #11 blades
metal-edged ruler
newspaper
acrylic tube paint, in dark green
paper plate
1 stencil brush, #5
clear spray varnish, mat or glossy finish (optional)

*If your chair has a slick or shiny white finish, remove the shine by either sanding it lightly or removing the existing finish with paint and varnish remover and painting it with white latex enamel paint.

Procedure:

1.   Enlarge all three stencil designs to size on the illustration board (see page 14), allowing at least 2 inches of space between designs. Tape both

Each square = 1 inch

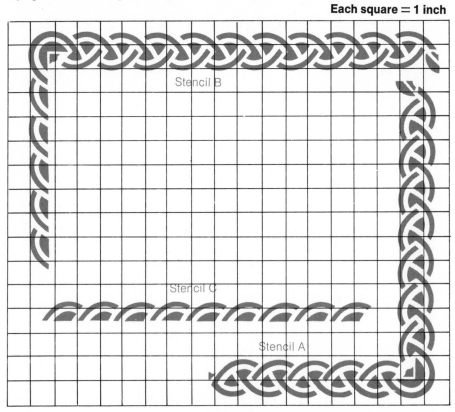

Stencil B

Stencil C

Stencil A

sheets of stencil paper over the designs so that you can cut them in duplicate; this will speed up the stenciling process. Using a fresh blade in your X-acto knife, cut out all the inner stencil openings; then, leaving a 1-inch border all around, use the ruler in combination with your knife to trim around each stencil design. Separate each pair of stencils, turn one of each pair over, and label each as shown.

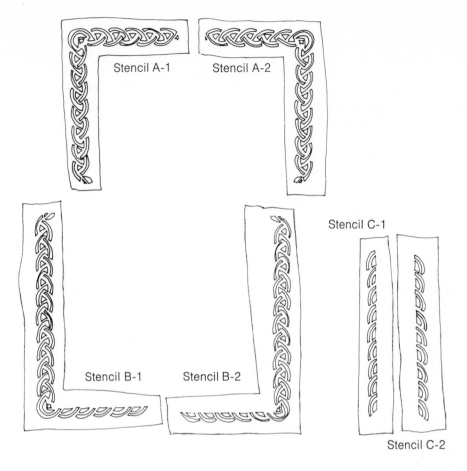

2.   Make sure that the surface of the chair you are using is clean, dry, and free of all wax and old varnish. Then cover a tabletop or other work surface with newspaper and lay the chair, folded flat, on top of it. The front side of the chair should be up.

3.   Position stencil A-1 on the chair as shown, and tape it into place. Make sure that it lies flat and is straight.

Squeeze a small amount of dark green paint onto a paper plate, and dip the tip of the stencil brush into it, removing the excess by pouncing the bristles on some newspaper. Using an up-and-down dabbing motion, apply the paint through all the openings until they are evenly coated with color. Then carefully lift up the stencil.

4.   Position stencil A-2 on the upper right-hand corner of the chair and tape it into place. Stencil the design, using the same technique described in step 3.

5.   Position stencil B-1 on the lower left-hand corner of the chair, tape it into place, and stencil the design.

6.   Complete the border framing the chair by positioning stencil B-2 on the lower right-hand corner, taping it in place, and stenciling the design.

7.   Allow the paint on the chair to dry for about 20 minutes, or until the design is dry to the touch. Turn the folded chair over so that the seat side is up. Notice that the chair seat is composed of six wooden slats with small spaces between each pair of slats. Position stencil C-1 just to the left of the center of the seat, tape it in place, and, using the same techniques outlined in step 3, stencil the design.

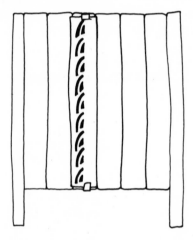

Remove the stencil and position it on the slat at the extreme right. Stencil the same design again.

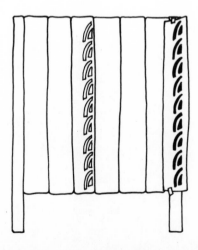

8.   Position stencil C-2 just to the right of the center of the seat, tape it in place, and stencil it. Repeat this design at the extreme left of the chair seat.

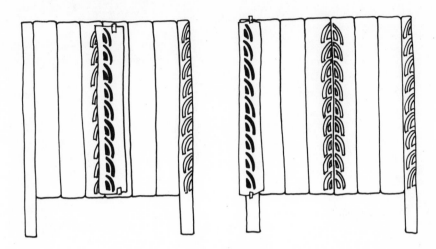

9.   For the final touch, place a strip of masking tape around the top of each slat, leaving ½ inch of the front end of the slat exposed.

Paint these exposed areas green. Let the paint dry and then carefully peel off the tape. Although acrylic paint dries fairly rapidly, it should set for 48 hours. If you wish to protect your chair further, spray it with a clear varnish in either a mat or glossy finish.

Hints and Ideas:

★This set of stencils can be used to make an enormous frame. Try using japan colors to stencil a frame around a large mirror, or use the design to border kitchen cabinets.

★Stencil an entire set of chairs and a table to match.

Planned Illusion Table

For friends who have an ultramodern apartment—a blend of glass, chrome, burled walnut, heavy, woven fabrics, and an occasional objet d'art—we created this somewhat facetious contemporary design: graphic, stenciled place settings.

The table looks great alone, but it looks sensational with clear glass plates bearing real green and white striped napkins and with real cutlery placed over the stenciled forks, knives, and spoons. Our friends tell us that the design not only adds cheer to their dining area, it also provides a stimulus for their two little girls' imaginations; aside from holding marathon make-believe tea parties, they've invented several games to play on the stenciled surface.

Tabletops offer great possibilities for design. Why not stencil one with your favorite game? A backgammon design or a checker/chess pattern with a fancy border would be both easy and eye-catching. Or, you can simulate the effect of expensive parquetry with stenciled designs.

Materials:

unfinished wooden parson's table, 30 inches square
latex enamel paint, in white
1 paintbrush, for enamel
5 pieces illustration board, each 15 by 20 inches
scissors
5 sheets stencil paper, each 18 by 24 inches
masking tape
#1 X-acto knife with #11 blades
marking pen
yardstick
soft lead pencil, #3B
acrylic tube paints, in orange, bright green, bright blue, bright red, and
    yellow
paper plates
5 stencil brushes, one #8 and four #5
newspaper

Procedure:

1.   Prepare the parson's table by painting it with the white latex enamel. Apply three coats in all, brushing the paint in a different direction for each coat. Allow the proper drying time between coats.

2.   Enlarge each of the five stencil designs to size on a separate illustration board (see page 14). Trim the sheets of stencil paper slightly smaller

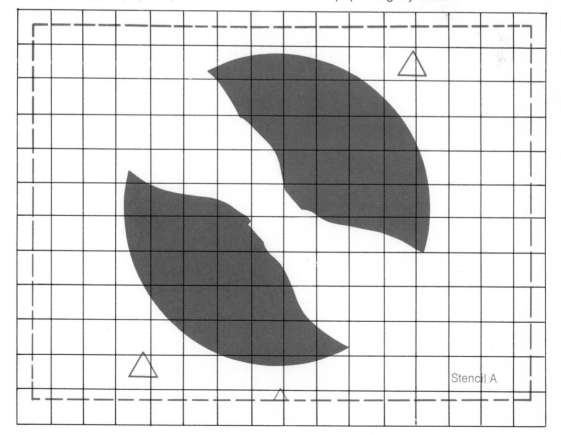

Stencil A

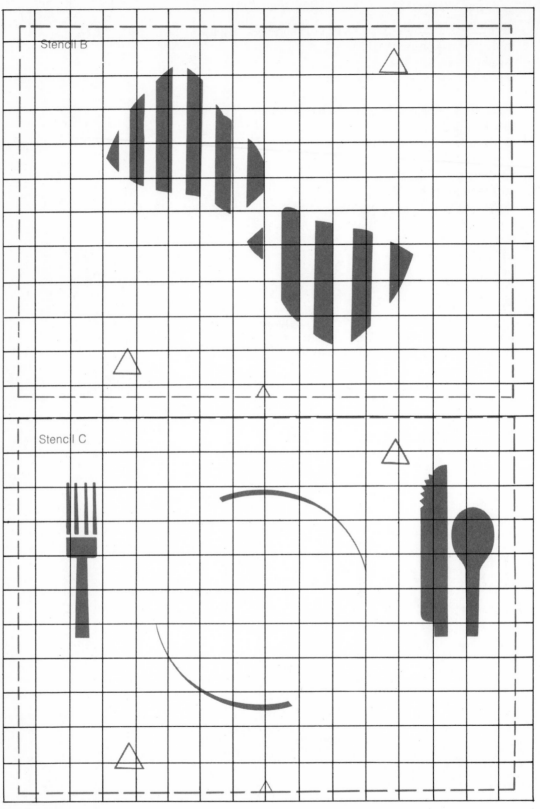

Each square = 1 inch

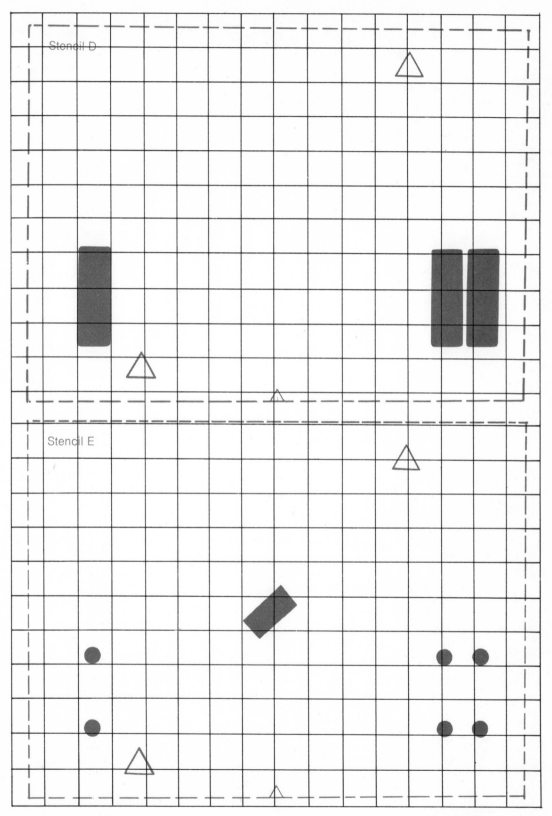

Stencil D

Stencil E

Each square = 1 inch

than the illustration board and then tape one piece over each design. Using a fresh blade in your X-acto knife, cut out each design and then cut around each design on the dotted line. Make sure that you have cut out the three triangles on each stencil, even though they are not part of the actual design; they are registration marks that will help you to line up each design on the tabletop as your stenciling progresses. Spread the stencils out flat in front of you and label each with a piece of masking tape and a marking pen.

3.   Using the yardstick, find and mark the center of each of the four sides of the table. Place stencil A on top of the table, making sure that the smallest triangle—the one at the bottom of the stencil—is centered directly over one of the pencil lines at the edge of the table.

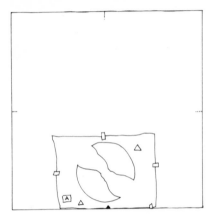

Tape the stencil in place. Then outline the registration marks—the two larger triangles—with the soft lead pencil.

4.   Squeeze a small amount of the orange paint onto a paper plate, dip the tip of a clean, dry #8 stencil brush into the paint, and remove the excess by pouncing the bristles on some newspaper. Keeping the edges of the stencil openings firmly pressed down with your fingers, apply the paint through the openings until all have been coated with a thin layer of paint—do *not* paint through the three triangular registration marks. Use an up-and-down dabbing motion to apply the paint. When finished, carefully remove the stencil and allow the design to dry.

5.   Use stencil A and the orange paint to repeat the same design three more times, each time centering the small triangle over the pencil lines on the table.

6.   Place stencil B on top of the table, centering the small triangle over one of the pencil lines at the edge of the table. Make sure that the two large triangles are directly over those already traced on the table.

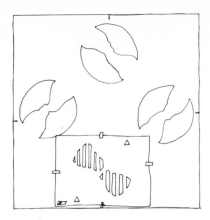

Using a clean, dry #5 stencil brush and the green paint on a **clean paper** plate, stencil this design on each of the four sides of the table. Follow the same stenciling procedure outlined in step 4. When you have completed stenciling the napkins, the table should look like this.

7.   Following the same exact procedure described in steps 3 and 4, add stencil C to the design with the blue paint and a clean, dry #5 stencil brush, then stencil D with the red paint and another #5 brush, and finally stencil E with the yellow paint and the remaining #5 brush. Then clean your brushes with water, allow the designs to dry for 24 hours, and remove the pencil marks with an eraser.

Hints and Ideas:

★Stencil these place settings directly on a cotton tablecloth or on washable fabric placemats, using acrylic paints.

★If you have a long parson's table of the sort used for buffets, stencil the four place settings in a row.

★These place settings stenciled on a picnic table would add fun to any backyard barbecue.

★If you wish, protect your stenciled tabletop with a coat of crystal-clear varnish, following manufacturer's instructions.

Early American Hardwood Floor

Not so long ago, when we owned a company that was young and suffering growing pains, we wanted to create a visually exciting showroom in which to impress buyers and publicists with the merits of our product. Our possibilities were limited by cost; we just couldn't afford to buy lots of sleek, prosperous-looking furniture and equipment. We decided to compensate for lack of cash with hard work and imagination.

The first step was to spend several days running around to all the secondhand office-furniture outlets in town. We bought several heavy wooden tables, an old desk, assorted wooden chairs, and other odds and ends. When we began stripping down the furniture, we made the happy discovery that two of the tables were solid oak. We revarnished some pieces and left others natural. Already a theme was being established: different varieties of old, smooth wood accessorized with baskets, trunks, and old drugstore counters—sort of an eclectic Provençal look.

Being the basis of our business, stenciling naturally played a great part in dressing up our decor. The first thing we decided to stencil was the hardwood floor. After designing a versatile geometric pattern that would work well with any additions to the room, we cut our stencils out of acetate. (Because of its durability, acetate is a good material to use whenever it's necessary to repeat the same design over and over.)

Our showroom was a smash. We stenciled other patterns on the walls, created parquet effects on the tabletops, wrote lots and lots of orders, and lived happily ever after.

Materials:

wooden floor
2 pieces illustration board, each 20 by 30 inches
chalk
yardstick
scissors
1 sheet .005 - gauge acetate,* 20 by 50 inches, clear
masking tape
#1 X-acto knife with #11 blades
metal-edged ruler
acrylic tube paints, in purple, yellow, and red
paper plates
3 stencil brushes, one #12,** one #8, and one #5
newspaper
liquid detergent
1 paintbrush, at least 3 inches wide
clear varnish

*If you use waxed stencil paper to cut your designs, cut several to allow for wear and tear.
**If you can't find a #12 stencil brush, try using a large glue brush.

Procedure:

1. Before you begin to stencil, you must prepare the floor. The best way to do this is to sand the floor down to bare wood. You can also paint the floor with a latex enamel—which will require a protective coating—in a color to match your room, or you can simply make sure that your floor is clean and dry and free from wax buildup. Use ammonia to remove any wax.

2. The next step is to calculate how many times you will need to repeat the stencil design to cover the area of the floor. To do this, we have devised the "box step." Cut a piece of illustration board to measure 15½ inches square. Make sure that this square is precise. Place the square in one corner of the room and, using the chalk, draw around it. Continue to mark off the square along two walls of the room, as shown.

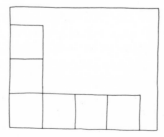

Measure how much space is left at the end of each row and divide each figure by 2. The result is the width of the borders that you must leave around the outside edges of the floor in order for the stenciled area of the floor to be centered. For instance, if 10 inches are left over at the end of one row and 12 at the end of the other, you will need to leave a 5-inch margin along the first wall and the wall opposite and a 6-inch margin along the remaining two walls. When you have arrived at your figures, erase the squares and then mark off your borders accordingly, drawing a guideline around the entire room with chalk and a yardstick. It is important that this guideline be straight and at right angles at the corners of the room.

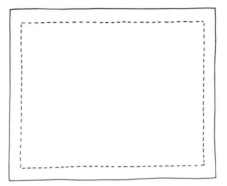

3.   Now position the square in one corner of the area you have marked off, making sure that two sides of it touch the guidelines. Trace around it with chalk. Working from left to right, repeat this process of tracing around the square until the entire floor has been marked off in squares.

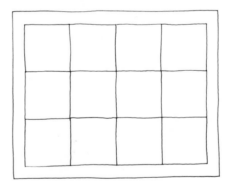

4.   Enlarge stencil A to size on the illustration board (see page 14). Rather than enlarging stencils B and C, simply draw on the illustration board two squares, one measuring 4 by 4 inches (stencil B) and one 2 by 2 inches (stencil C). Allow at least 2 inches of space between each of the designs. Trim the acetate so that it is slightly smaller than the illustration board and tape it over the designs. Using the X-acto knife and a metal-edged ruler to guide the blade, cut out the designs and then cut around the designs, allowing at least a 1-inch border all around.

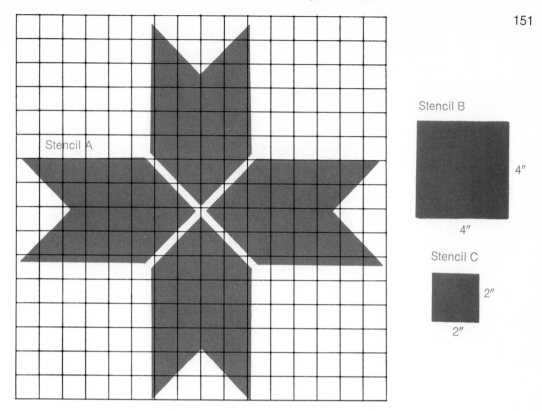

Stencil B

4″

4″

Stencil C

2″

2″

Stencil A

5. The first step in the stenciling process is to repeat stencil A in each of the squares traced on the floor. Tape stencil A in place as shown, taking care that the stencil is well centered in the square.

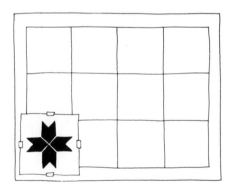

Squeeze a small amount of purple paint onto a paper plate, dip the tip of the #12 stencil brush into the paint, and remove the excess by pouncing the bristles on some newspaper. Keeping the edges of the stencil openings firmly pressed down with your fingers as you stencil, apply the paint through the stencil openings until all have been thoroughly coated. Use an up-and-down dabbing motion and work from the edges of the design toward the center. Remove the tape and carefully lift the stencil. Let dry.

6.   Center stencil A in the next square and, using the same procedure described in step 5, stencil the design. Continue stenciling the squares with stencil A, working from left to right, until all the squares are completed, taking care that each time the design is repeated, it is centered in the square. When paint starts to build up in the stencil brush, stop immediately and wash the brush with liquid detergent and warm water; rinse it well and allow it to dry before you proceed. You may also need to wash the stencil.

7.   Tape stencil B into place on one of the squares, making sure that the chalk marks intersect in the center of the design.

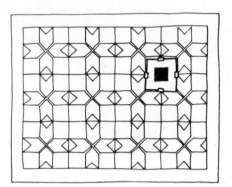

Using yellow paint on a clean paper plate and the #8 stencil brush, stencil the design according to the procedure described in step 5. Repeat stencil B in each square on the floor.

8.   Tape stencil C in place as shown.

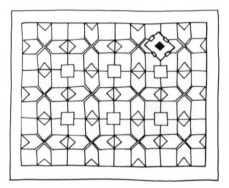

Using the red paint on another paper plate and the #5 stencil brush, add stencil C to each square of the floor, using the same procedures described in step 5.

9.   Allow the completed floor to dry for 24 hours. Then, following manufacturer's directions, apply a coat of varnish. When it is thoroughly dry, apply a second coat. For a beautiful sheen, add a third and a fourth coat.

Water Lily Treasure Box

The inspiration for this project came through the mail. We received a letter from a fellow designer, an art director at an ad agency. After discussing several business points, the letter concluded:

"This letter may appear to be tear-stained. It's not. It's just that I've had a very wet week. As of Monday, it had been raining for five days. Tuesday morning my waterbed sprang a leak, and then the washer overflowed, flooding everything the bed hadn't. I spent all that day working on an ad for club soda that featured a cascading waterfall. That night I watched a Jacques Yves Cousteau special, *Mr. Peabody and the Mermaid,* and *The Creature from the Black Lagoon.*

"When I opened my mail Wednesday morning and found a religious tract that recited the story of Jonah and the whale, I began to suspect something was fishy. Was some drip applying the old Chinese water torture? That evening I turned on my TV just as Esther Williams was floating into a grand finale scene on a giant water lily; ever since, I've been having dreams about giant water lilies that like to sing and dance.

"I'm afraid the dam has burst. My girlfriend has taken up scuba diving, my doctor has put me on a liquid diet, and my analyst suggests a Caribbean cruise to get away from it all. Buddies, can you spare a towel?"

Materials:
unfinished wooden box*
newspaper
fine steel wool
acrylic tube paints, in turquoise dark green, white, and bright pink
paper plates
1 paintbrush, 1 inch wide, for painting the box
1 piece illustration board, 15 by 20 inches
scissors
1 sheet stencil paper, 18 by 24 inches
masking tape
#1 X-acto knife with #11 blades
3 stencil brushes, one #5 and two #1
clear, high-gloss varnish
1 paintbrush, for varnish

*Our box measured 5 inches deep, 8 inches wide, and 3 inches high.

Procedure:

1. Cover your work surface with newspaper to prepare for finishing the wooden box. Using fine steel wool, rub the box inside and out until it is smooth. Then squeeze about 3 tablespoons of turquoise paint onto a paper plate and, using a brush, blend in a bit of water, adding more water until the consistency of the paint is that of heavy cream. Using the 1-inch paintbrush, evenly coat the box—inside and out—with paint and let it dry for about 30 minutes. Add a second coat of paint and allow that to dry for at least an hour. When the box is completely dry, it will be ready to stencil.

2. Enlarge each of the three stencil designs on the illustration board (see page 14), allowing at least 2 inches space between designs. Trim the stencil paper slightly smaller than the illustration board, and tape it in place over the designs. Then cut the stencils, using the X-acto knife. Finally, cut out each design by cutting along the dotted line. If you purchased a box that is the same size as ours, the cutout stencils will fit exactly over the top of the box, making the job of stenciling it easier. If the box is a different size, you'll have to center the designs.

3. Position stencil A on top of the box as shown, and tape it into place.

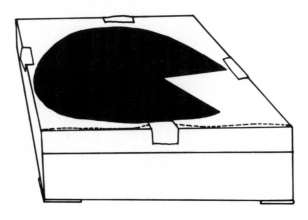

Stencil A

Stencil B

Stencil C

Each square = 1 inch

Squeeze a small amount of dark green paint onto a paper plate, dip the tip of the #5 stencil brush into the paint, and remove the excess by pouncing the bristles on some newspaper. Keeping the edges of the stencil firmly pressed down with your fingers as you stencil, apply the paint through the stencil opening with an up-and-down dabbing motion. When the opening has been evenly coated with paint, remove the stencil and let the design dry to the touch.

4.   Position stencil B directly over the lily pad you have just stenciled and tape it into place as shown.

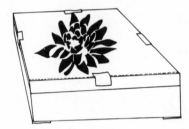

Squeeze a bit of white paint onto a clean paper plate and, using a #1 stencil brush, stencil the design, using the same technique as you did in step 3. Without removing the stencil, allow the design to dry.

5.   Squeeze a bit of bright pink paint onto the same paper plate and mix it in with the white to make a pastel shade of pink. Dip the tip of a #1 brush into the paint and remove all the excess by pouncing the brush on newspaper. The brush should be very dry because you will not be adding much color in this step. Following the illustration, add a bit of pink toward the center of each flower petal, fading it out toward the tip. Remove the stencil and let the design dry.

6.   Place stencil C over the middle of the stenciled lily design and tape it into place. This unusual little shape will give your flower a center. Stencil the design with a #1 stencil brush and bright pink acrylic paint. Remove the stencil and let the design dry for 24 hours. Clean your brushes with water.

7.   Following manufacturer's instructions, coat the finished box with varnish and allow it to dry. Repeat with a second coat if you wish.

Pine Plank Placemats

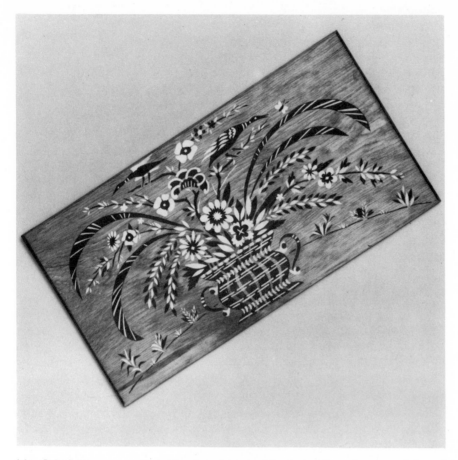

Mr. Grimbel was our neighborhood eccentric as well as the proprietor of the local lumberyard. Though he worked in the yard all day long, he was never much concerned with customers. He was preoccupied with other matters, such as concocting his own wood stains and skillfully whittling miniature soldiers and horses, which he gave to all of us, the children who loved his funny ways.

One day Mr. Grimbel invited six or seven of us to have lunch with him and his wife in their huge frame house, surrounded by eucalyptus trees. As we were led through the house by Mrs. Grimbel, a perfect Mrs. Santa Claus, we stared wide-eyed at the amazing wooden objects that seemed to fill every room. She seated us at a gigantic table made from petrified redwood. The placemats she put before us were handpainted and made of wood. The plates were wooden, and the goblets were wooden; the food, thank goodness, was not.

Wooden placemats are surprisingly practical. They can hold a sizzling hot dish, they can be washed clean, and they'll last for years and years. An inexpensive gift, an instant heirloom, these Americana placemats will dress up any table and make every meal seem hearty and heartwarming.

Materials:

1 piece pine,* 1 inch thick, 12 by 21½ inches, with beveled edges**
newspaper
wood stain, medium shade
1 paintbrush, 1 inch wide
2 pieces illustration board, each 20 by 30 inches
masking tape
2 sheets stencil paper, each 18 by 24 inches
#1 X-acto knife with #11 blades
4 pushpins *or* thumbtacks
tailor's chalk
acrylic tube paints, in brown and white
paper plates
2 stencil brushes, both #5

*If you want to make a set of placemats, buy four pieces of pine instead of one.
**Ask your lumberman to bevel the edges, or sand them yourself until they are smooth.

Procedure:

1.   Spread a layer of newspaper over a work surface and lay the pine piece on top. Following manufacturer's instructions, apply a coat of wood stain to all sides of the pine piece, using the paintbrush.

2.   Enlarge both stencil designs to size on a separate piece of illustration board (see page 14). Tape a sheet of stencil paper over each of the designs, and, using the X-acto knife, cut them out; then cut around the designs, allowing a 1-inch margin. Make sure that you have cut out the four triangles on each stencil, even though they are not part of the actual design; they are registration marks that will help you to line up each design as you stencil.

3.   Center stencil A on top of the placemat and pin it into place with the pushpins or the thumbtacks. Outline the four registration marks with the tailor's chalk.

4.   Squeeze a small amount of the brown paint onto a paper plate, dip the tip of one of the stencil brushes into the paint, and remove the excess from the brush by pouncing it on some newspaper. Keeping the edges of the stencil openings firmly pressed down with your fingers, apply the paint through the stencil openings. Using an up-and-down dabbing motion, stencil until all the openings have been coated with a thin layer of paint. Do *not* apply paint through the triangular registration marks—their only purpose is to show you where to place stencil B. Carefully remove the stencil and let the design dry.

5.   Position stencil B on top of the placemat, making sure that the registration marks are aligned with the chalk marks. Pin the stencil in place. Using white paint and a clean, dry stencil brush, stencil the design, following the same procedure described in step 4. Remove the stencil and let the design dry. Remove the marks made by the tailor's chalk with a damp sponge, and wash your brushes.

Stencil A

Stencil B

Each square = 1 inch

Amerindian Matchstick Blind

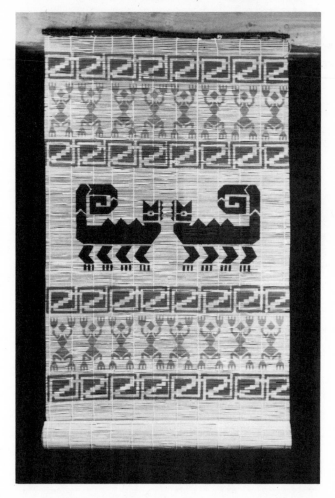

Centuries of sophisticated cultures—some anthropologists estimate more than twelve thousand year's worth—existed in North America before European colonization of the continent. This project celebrates the art of those first Americans, the Indians. Their art was rich in symbolism and was closely intertwined with a complicated religion that sustained them in the arduous task of living with the land they loved.

We've chosen three traditional designs for this project and used them to embellish inexpensive, matchstick window shades. Indians obtained their colors from the earth—hematite for red, copper ores for blue, and rich clays for brown and black. Today, these colors have been duplicated in acrylic paints.

Since this stencil project is a modular one, you'll be able to decorate window shades of any size. If you don't have shades of the matchstick variety, ordinary white ones will work just as well.

Materials:

matchstick shade, 2 by 3 feet
1 piece illustration board, 15 by 20 inches
scissors
1 sheet stencil paper, 18 by 24 inches
masking tape
#1 X-acto knife with #11 blades
metal-edged ruler
marking pen
newspaper
pencil
acrylic tube paints, in rust, turquoise, and dark brown
paper plates
3 stencil brushes, all #5

Procedure:

1.   Enlarge each of the three stencil designs to size on the illustration board (see page 14), allowing at least 2 inches of space between designs.

Each square = 1 inch

Cut the stencil paper slightly smaller than the illustration board and tape it in place over the designs. Cut out the stencil designs with the X-acto knife, using a ruler to guide the blade. Leaving at least a 1-inch margin, cut around each design and remove it from the board. Using small pieces of masking tape and a marking pen, label each design.

2.   Spread a layer of newspaper over a work surface large enough to accommodate the window shade laid out flat. Measure 2 inches down from the top of the window shade and make a few pencil lines to indicate where to begin stenciling. Tape stencil A into place as shown, making sure that the left side of the design almost touches the left edge of the shade and that the top of the design runs along the pencil lines.

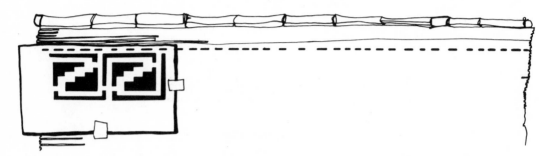

3.   Squeeze a small amount of rust-colored paint onto a paper plate. Dip the tip of a stencil brush into the paint, and remove the excess by pouncing the bristles on newspaper until the brush is fairly dry. Pressing down the edges of the stencil openings with your fingers, apply the paint through the openings, using an up-and-down motion. When all the openings have been colored in, remove the tape and carefully lift off the stencil.

4.   Re-use stencil A to repeat the design three more times across the top of the shade as shown, making sure that the top of the design always runs along the pencil lines.

Each time that you begin a design repeat, tape the stencil in place, apply the rust-colored paint, and then reposition the stencil.

5.   Center stencil B directly below the first design you made with stencil A, and tape it in place. Using a clean, dry stencil brush and the turquoise paint, stencil the design, using the technique described in step 3. Re-use stencil B to repeat the design three more times across the top.

6.   Re-use stencil A to add another row of designs directly below the row

that you just stenciled; stencil them with the rust-colored paint.

7. Mark the center of the window shade with a pencil. Then position stencil C 1 inch to the left of that center mark and tape the stencil in place. Using the dark brown acrylic paint and a clean, dry stencil brush, stencil in the designs.

8. When stencil C is completely dry, turn it over. It should now be positioned, as shown, to make a reverse design. Tape it in place 1 inch to the right of the center mark and then stencil it with the dark brown paint; remove the stencil.

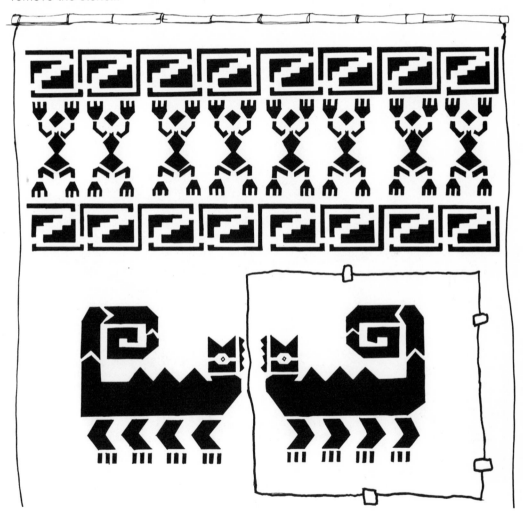

9. Using stencil A, then B, then A again, stencil a border below the two animal designs (stencil C) that is exactly like the border at the top of the shade. Then wash your brushes in water, erase any remaining pencil marks, and allow the paint to dry completely before hanging the shade.

Hints and Ideas:

★Since these stencils are modular, you can mix and match to create your own variation of an Indian design.

5
Mixed
Media

All surfaces should be clean and dry before stenciling. Unless otherwise noted, it is not necessary to add a protective coating. *Cement; concrete; asphalt:* Stencil with acrylics, spray paints, deck paints, or oil-based paints. *Ceramics, glazed and fired:* Avoid ceramics intended for use with food or on floors. Stencil with japan colors only. *Ceramics, unglazed and fired:* Surface may first be painted with acrylic or latex paints. Stencil with acrylics, latex paints, or japan colors. *Cork paneling; fiber board; bulletin boards:* Stencil with acrylics, latex paints, or spray paints. *Fibers, natural woven:* Stencil woven fibers, such as sea grass, coco fiber, etc., with acrylics, spray paints, or latex paints. *Floor tiles:* Stencil with acrylics, spray paints, or deck paints. Protect with two or more coats of a *clear floor varnish. Glass and mirrors:* Clean first with any glass cleaner. Stencil with japan colors only. *Leather:* Surface can first be stained with leather dye. Stencil with acrylics. Protect the final design with leather finisher. *Metal, galvanized:* Before stenciling, spray lightly with a clear mat fixative or paint with enamel paints or japan colors. Stencil with acrylics, enamel paints, or japan colors. Protect the final design by spraying lightly with a transparent fixative. *Metal, painted:* On flat finishes, stencil with acrylics; on shiny finishes, with japan colors. Use engine enamel to stencil on stoves. *Metal, shiny:* Stencil only with japan colors. *Plasterboard:* Paint first with flat latex or latex enamel; let dry. Stencil with acrylics, permanent marking pens, latex paints, spray paints, japan colors, or sizing for gold leaf. *Plastics, nonshiny:* Stencil with acrylics when possible; test by applying paint to the bottom of the object, allowing it to dry for 48 hours, and scratching it lightly with a fingernail. If the paint scratches away easily, stencil with japan colors. *Plastics, shiny:* Stencil only with japan colors.

Dutch Girl Serving Tray

Although we've never been to Holland, it has become the subject of a very pleasant fantasy. We always imagine everyone there to be either young, blond, and healthy or older, peaceful, and content, like a movie version of the perfect grandparents. One's daily tasks in this naïve fantasy consist of growing tulips, watching windmills, or figuring out new ways to hold back the sea. Everyone bustles about in traditional costumes and wooden shoes, and when all the apple-cheeked Netherlanders sit down to a meal, it invariably consists of rich, dark chocolate and steaming cups of black coffee. Mainly, everyone is happy, vice is nonexistent, skies are always blue with puffy white clouds, and peace and contentment eternally prevail; pure, unadulterated, unworldly fantasy. To preserve this fantasy, we may never visit Holland.

We've decorated a large metal tray with a delft-blue design of a happy little Dutch girl on her way home with a bundle of firewood. The effect is contemporary with just a touch of nice nostalgia. This is an exceptionally easy project: one stencil, one color. Use the tray as a coffee server, as a dessert tray for a lavish chocolate pie or a batch of creamy fudge, or as an emergency dinner tray. People are bound to be charmed by this pretty little Dutch girl, who will unfailingly help make a smile a part of every meal.

Materials:
round metal tray, 20 inches in diameter
1 piece illustration board, 15 by 20 inches
scissors
1 sheet stencil paper, 18 by 24 inches
masking tape
#1 X-acto knife with #11 blades
newspaper
1 can (16 ounces) spray paint, in flat white
acrylic tube paints, in cobalt blue and white
paper plate
1 stencil brush, #5

Procedure:

1. Enlarge the stencil design to size on the illustration board (see page 14). Trim the stencil paper so that it is slightly smaller than the illustration

Each square = 1 inch

board and tape it in place over the design. Using the X-acto knife, cut the stencil, doing first the branches because they are the most delicate element of the design. When you have cut out all the inner designs, trim around the stencil, leaving at least a 1-inch border all around.

2. Spread a layer of newspaper out under the tray, and, following manufacturer's instructions, spray the tray with the flat white paint. Let it dry thoroughly.

3. Tape the stencil to the tray, making sure that it is centered. Squeeze a small amount of the blue paint onto a paper plate and add a very small amount of white acrylic paint; using a brush, mix them until they are thoroughly blended. Remember that acrylic paints appear lighter in color when they are wet than they do when dry. Dip the tip of the stencil brush into the paint, and remove the excess by pouncing the bristles on some newspaper. Keeping the edges of the stencil openings pressed down with your fingers, apply the paint through the stencil openings, using an up-and-down dabbing motion. When all the openings have been coated with paint, carefully remove the stencil and let the design dry. Wash the brush with water.

Hints and Ideas:

★Place this stencil over the top of a chocolate sheet cake and lightly sift confectioners sugar through the openings. When all the openings have been coated, carefully lift the stencil straight up to avoid smudging the edges.

★Try stenciling this design on the front of a cotton apron, using acrylic paints.

★Stencil this design on round, nonplastic canisters by wrapping it around a canister, taping it in place, and then stenciling it with acrylic paints.

Old-Fashioned Tea Rose Trunk

Have you ever had the delightful experience of climbing a narrow flight of stairs and discovering a small door that led to a musty, forgotten attic; one filled with a jumbled assortment of old wardrobe chests and dusty trunks? If so, you'll remember the excitement of being alone in the midst of all that antique richness. Time seems to dissolve as you open the first trunk and begin to sort through its contents: yellowed packets of old love letters tied together with faded ribbons, crumpled satin-and-lace wedding dresses that evoke visions of wasp-waisted Gibson girls, and Moroccan leather scrapbooks with dog-eared pages of brittle photographs of picnics and buggy rides that seemingly took place in an age when days were longer and life itself was a more tranquil proposition.

In honor of peaceful, happy hours spent in remembrance of things past, we've created a design to stencil on a trunk; a trunk in which you may wish to start saving your own mementos. And perhaps someday someone will discover it, linger over its contents, and wistfully wish for the peaceful, happy time that was the twentieth century.

Materials:

a trunk*
1 piece illustration board, 20 by 30 inches
2 sheets stencil paper, each 18 by 24 inches
masking tape
#1 X-acto knife with #11 blades
scissors
marking pen
newspaper
acrylic tube paints, in dark pink, green, yellow, and blue
paper plates
4 stencil brushes, all #4

*Ours measured 12 inches in height, 16 inches in width, and 31 inches in length, but you can use this design on any trunk by adjusting the number of repetitions of the modular stencils. The trunk we bought was all black, but we painted it three colors with acrylic paints; the top was painted pastel pink (obtained by mixing dark pink and white), the narrow strip below the top was painted pale yellow (obtained by mixing yellow and white), and the remainder of the trunk was painted powder blue (obtained by mixing blue and white). This design, however, will look fine on a plain trunk.

Procedure:

1. Enlarge all twelve designs to size on the illustration board (see page 14), leaving at least 2 inches between designs. Tape one sheet of stencil paper over the designs and, using the X-acto knife, cut as many stencils from it as you can; remove it, tape the second sheet over the remaining designs, and cut them out. Then cut out all the stencils with scissors, allowing at least a 1-inch border all around. With small pieces of masking tape and a marking pen, label each stencil.

2. On a work surface or floor, spread a layer of newspaper. You will first stencil the ends of the trunk; set the trunk on one end so that the other end is facing you. Onto three separate paper plates, squeeze small amounts of dark pink, green, and yellow paints. As you stencil, keep adding small amounts of paints to the paper plates as needed.

3. Position stencils A, B-1, and B-2 on the end of the trunk as shown, and tape them into place.

Dip the tip of one of the brushes into the green paint, and remove the excess by pouncing the bristles on some newspaper. Apply the paint through stencils B-1 and B-2 with an up-and-down dabbing motion until all the stencil openings have been coated with a thin layer of paint.

Stencil A

Stencil B-1   Stencil B-2

Stencil C

Stencil D

Stencil E

Stencil H

Stencil F   Stencil I

Stencil G

Stencil J-1   Stencil J-2

Each square = 1 inch

4. Using the same stenciling procedure described in step 3, follow the color-coded illustration and stencil each of the openings of stencil A with the appropriate color.

Yellow Green Pink

When you have stenciled the designs on this end of the trunk, remove the stencils and let the paint set until dry to the touch. Then reposition the trunk so that the opposite end is facing up. Repeat the same designs—stencils A, B-1, and B-2—and the same stenciling procedures to complete the second end.

5. To create the fern border on the front of the trunk, use stencils B-1 and B-2 in the positions shown.

Use the same green paint and the same stenciling procedures given in step 3.

6. Position stencil C as shown in Figure A of the illustration. Fill in the stencil openings with color, using the same stenciling technique described in step 3 and following the color coding in Figure B of the illustration.

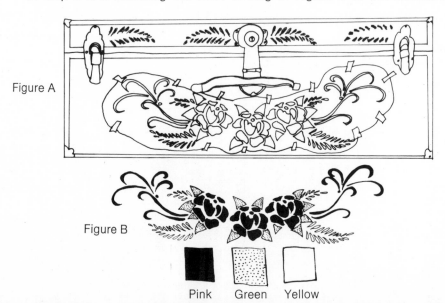

Figure A

Figure B

Pink   Green   Yellow

When all the designs have been stenciled on the front of the trunk, remove the stencils and allow the design to dry.

7. To "build" the pattern on the top of the trunk, begin by positioning stencil D in the lower left-hand corner of the trunk top, as shown.

Onto a clean paper paint, squeeze a small amount of blue paint. Using a clean, dry brush and the same procedures described in step 3, stencil the design. When all the openings have been filled with color, remove the stencil, reposition it, and stencil the design again. Continue repositioning and stenciling until a complete pattern has been created, as shown.

8. Using stencil E and the dark pink paint, stencil the rose in all the positions shown.

9. Using stencil F-1 and the yellow paint, stencil daisies in all the positions shown.

When all the daisies have been stenciled, use stencils G, H, and I, in that order, to stencil the centers of all the daisies. Follow the same stenciling procedures given in step 3, and follow the color-coded illustration.

Green

Yellow

Pink

10. Finally, use stencils J-1 and J-2 and the green paint to randomly stencil leaves on the top of the trunk. The illustration shows how we placed ours.

We overlapped the stencils over the roses and stenciled through them, fading out the green paint as it reached the dark pink petals. We also stenciled clusters of leaves around the outside edges of the trunk top, overlapping them to create a dense-foliage effect. When you've finished this step, the trunk is completed.

Art Deco Auto

Our friend Melissa is a beautiful, talented young woman. By day, she is a successful businesswoman; by night, a glamorous siren of the 1930s, an era she believes to have been the highpoint of American design, culture, and refinement.

Evenings, Melissa is always clothed in antique dresses and gowns, veils, and foxes. Her apartment is a sumptuous mélange of blue mirror, low *moderne* shell sofas and chairs, and accordianed Deco screens that gleam with layers of Oriental lacquer. An evening with Melissa is truly an experience to remember: melodic strains from Cole Porter, cocktails from frosted Deco goblets, and then a spin around town in her 1930 Model A coupe.

Obviously, we don't expect everyone to have a Model A. This design, however, will work well on any car. If you prefer your designs to be stationary, use this border on a wall, a floor, or even notepaper.

Materials:

an antique automobile,* in a dark color
1 piece illustration board, 20 by 30 inches
masking tape
2 sheets stencil paper, each 18 by 24 inches
#1 X-acto knife with #11 blades
metal-edged ruler
marking pen, in black
grease pencil, in white
plastic spoon
½ pint japan color, in white
paper plates
1 stencil brush, #5
scissors
turpentine

*Ours was a 1930 Model A Ford. You could, of course, use a brand new car. If the color of your car is light, simply stencil with a dark paint.

Procedure:

1.   Enlarge the stencil design to size on the illustration board (see page 14), and tape one sheet of stencil paper over the design. Using the X-acto

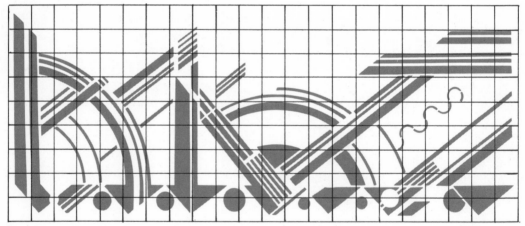

Each square = 1 inch

knife, cut the stencil. Use the metal-edged ruler to guide the blade as you cut the straight lines, and go slowly to avoid cutting bridges (see page 19 for stencil repair). Remove the stencil from the board and, with a small piece of masking tape and a marking pen, label it A. Tape the second sheet of stencil paper over the design, cut it out, and remove it from the board. Then turn it over and label it B.

2.   Make sure that the car you are working on is clean, dry, and free of wax. Then choose a flat surface on which to stencil—the design is too delicate to be effective around curves—and mark off on it a series of dots that, if connected, would make a line that is straight and parallel to the lower edge of the body of the car. Use a ruler to measure and a grease pencil to make the dots. Using the dots as a guide, place a strip of tape just above them. The tape will serve as a guide for the placement of the stencil.

3. Tape stencil A in place, as shown.

Using the plastic spoon, scoop about a tablespoon of paint out onto a paper plate. (Because japan paints dry so quickly, it is best to work with small amounts at a time. Leave the spoon in the paint to scoop out more paint as needed.) Then dip the tip of the stencil brush into the paint and remove the excess by pouncing the bristles on a clean area of the plate. Remember that japan paint is of a thin consistency; consequently, to prevent the paint from running under the stencil and ruining the design, the brush should be fairly dry and contain very little paint. Keeping the stencil bridges firmly pressed down with the tip of a pencil, apply the paint through the openings with an up-and-down dabbing motion—do not stroke. Apply the paint very thinly since you will be adding a second coat. When the first coat has been applied, leave the stencil in place and allow the paint to dry to the touch. Under normal circumstances, this will take about 5 minutes. Then, using the same procedure, apply the second coat and let it dry before going on to the next step.

4. Reposition the stencil as shown in the illustration. Make sure that the openings on the left-hand side of the stencil fit close to the right-hand side of the design previously stenciled. Notice that the stencil has been placed right over the door seam.

Using the same procedure outlined in step 3, stencil the design.

5. To complete the border on our car, it was necessary to cut away a portion of the stencil so that it looked like Figure A of the illustration. (Since cars differ, you may be able to eliminate this procedure.) To do this, place pieces of tape on the stencil and then cut off the area indicated by the dotted line.

Figure A

Figure B

Now position the altered stencil on the car as shown in Figure B of the illustration, making sure that the design fits closely to the design you have just stenciled. Using the same stenciling procedures described in step 3, apply two coats of paint through the openings.

6. To stencil the other side of the car, repeat the same procedures given in steps 2 through 5, but use stencil B. When the design is finished, clean your brush with turpentine.

Hints and Ideas:

★If the space you are stenciling is longer or shorter than ours, adjust the design by increasing or decreasing the number of times it is repeated.

Mediterranean Floor Tiles

Our operatic friend Theodora, an aspiring diva and an aficionado of every-thing Italian (pasta, Pisa, pizza, pinches, etc.), always wanted a floor tiled with those beautiful, handpainted Mediterranean tiles. And she was deter-mined to have such a floor until she priced the tiles and realized that one's got to *own* the Mediterranean to be able to afford them. When Theodora ended up buying one tile to use as a trivet, we explained how easy it is to capture the beauty of handpainted tiles using inexpensive materials.

With spray paint and stencils, Theodora became a quick-change artist, rapidly transforming plain, self-adhesive floor tiles into richly dec-orated replicas of handcrafted Mediterranean tiles. With a little help from her friends, she completely changed the look of her living/dining area in two days.

Not only is it possible to turn an ordinary floor into a masterpiece of interlocking patterns, it's just as easy to tile an uninteresting wall, disguise a stained counter, revamp a tabletop, or dramatize a ceiling. All you need is a bit of money, some time, and a desire to make a glamorous change in your environment.

By the way, our friend Theodora, always a bit inclined to excess, has gone on to more ambitious projects. In fact, almost every available surface in her apartment has been covered with stenciled designs. On a still night, if you listen carefully, you just may be able to hear her singing a fiery aria from *Carmen,* accompanied by the staccato beat of her stencil brush.

Materials:

smooth-surfaced adhesive-backed floor tiles,* each 12 inches square
4 pieces illustration board, each 15 by 20 inches
scissors
8 sheets stencil paper, each 18 by 24 inches
masking tape
#1 X-acto knife with #11 blades
marking pen
newspaper
nonpermanent spray adhesive
enamel spray paint, in bright blue, pineapple yellow, bright orange, and
jungle green
paint thinner *or* turpentine
paper towels
rubber cement thinner
clear protective finish, such as polyurethane
1 paintbrush, 3 inches wide

*If you are planning to stencil more than nine tiles (3 square feet), speed up the process by cutting more stencils.

Procedure:

1. Enlarge each of the four stencil designs to size on separate pieces of illustration board (see page 14). Cut the sheets of stencil paper slightly smaller than the illustration boards and tape two of them over each design. (As you stencil, you will alternate stencils in each pair to allow the paint on the one just used to dry.) Using a fresh blade in your X-acto knife, cut out each stencil design and then cut around each stencil, leaving at least a 1-inch border all around. Make sure that you cut out the four small triangles on each stencil, even though they are not part of the design; they are registration marks that will help you to line up each design on the tile as needed. Label each stencil with a piece of masking tape and marking pen.

2. Spread a large area with newspaper to make a drying area for the tiles, and cover a table in a well-ventilated area with newspaper to make a work space. (You can do this outdoors on a nice day.) Then lightly spray the backs of stencils A-1 and A-2 with adhesive and let them dry until just slightly sticky. Position stencil A-1 on the first tile, sticky side against the tile and all four registration marks aligned on all four edges of the tile.

Stencil A   Stencil B

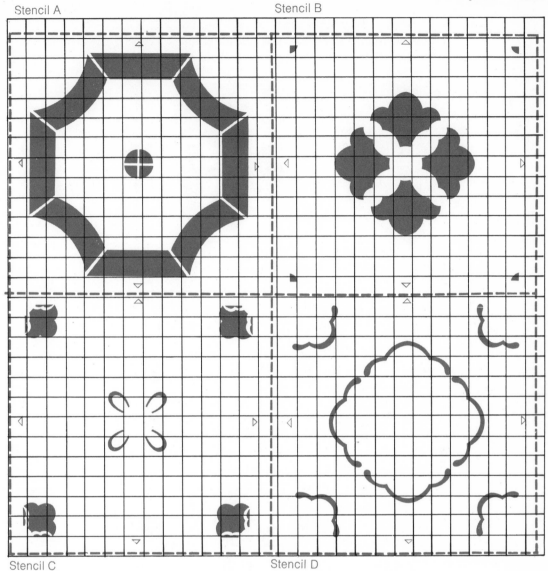

Stencil C   Stencil D

When the design is properly positioned, press down the edges of the stencil until they lightly adhere to the tile. Holding the can of blue spray paint about 12 inches above the tile and at a slight angle to it, lightly spray through the stencil openings until all the exposed areas of the tile are covered with paint. (Do *not* spray heavily; if you do, the stencil will take too long to dry before it can be used again.) Then carefully lift the stencil straight up from the tile to prevent smudging the paint. Lay the tile flat on the drying area to dry. Also set stencil A-1 aside to dry, making sure that it lies flat.

3. Following the same procedure given in step 2 but using stencil A-2, stencil the second tile. Stencil the third tile with stencil A-1, which should be dry by now. Continue stenciling the blue designs in this manner until all the tiles have been completed. Additional spray adhesive should be used whenever needed to keep the backs of the stencils slightly sticky.

4. When all the tiles are completely dry, use stencils B-1 and B-2 with the yellow paint to add the next design element. Use the same stenciling procedure that is described in step 2. Your tiles should now look like this.

5. When the tiles are dry, apply the next design by using stencils C-1 and C-2 and the orange spray paint, following the same stenciling procedure given in step 2. The tiles should now look like this.

6. Using the same procedure, add stencils D-1 and D-2 to the tiles with green spray paint. The tiles should now look like this.

7.   Clean your hands with paint thinner or turpentine and allow the tiles to dry for 24 hours. Then dip a paper towel in the rubber cement thinner and wipe away the accumulated spray adhesive from the surface of the tiles. (The thinner will not damage the paint or the tiles.) With the tiles still on the newspaper, brush over each tile a coat of clear polyurethane-type finish, following manufacturer's instructions. Since some finishes are not as transparent as others, test yours first before you apply it. Let the finish dry thoroughly, and apply a second coat. When the second coat is completely dry, peel off the backing from the tiles and press them into place on a clean, dry surface.

Hints and Ideas:

★Cover a piece of plywood with the tiles and set it on a base of some sort to make a beautiful handcrafted coffee table.

★If any smudges have been made on the stenciled tiles, remove them with a razor blade after the paint has dried but before the finish has been applied.

★Translate this project into an already existing linoleum floor.

Heavenly Huge Hopscotch

Since children spend a great deal of time immersed in a world of fantasy, we felt it only appropriate to create a fanciful design for them. To replace chalky, smudgy hopscotches, we've designed a lovely, lacy one that you can stencil on a sidewalk, patio, driveway, or garage floor. It's also perfect to add a touch of whimsy to a game-room floor, where it will come in handy for rainy-day indoor sports.

If you tire of hopscotch, move on to other large-scale games. Once you've read Chapter 1 and learned how simple it is to enlarge any design, you can translate any tabletop game into a huge supergraphic for a floor.

You could, for example, stencil a large checkerboard; gather a group of people together to become human checkers, leapfrogging over one another. The same applies to backgammon, Parcheesi, chess, and many other games. Of course, whether or not you ever actually use your stenciled game—whether it's our hopscotch or a design of your own—the design will add a spark of interest to any setting.

Materials:

any smooth paved surface, such as cement, concrete, flagstone, or
    asphalt, at least 3 by 10 feet
2 pieces illustration board, each 20 by 30 inches
scissors
2 sheets stencil paper, each 18 by 24 inches
masking tape
#1 X-acto knife with #11 blades
yardstick
colored chalk
acrylic tube paints, in red, sky blue, bright pink, bright green, orange,
    purple, and cobalt blue
paper plates
7 stencil brushes, one #8 and six #12*
newspaper

*If you can't find #12 stencil brushes, try using large glue brushes.

Procedure:

1.   Enlarge the border design to size on one piece of illustration board
and the nine numerals on the other (see page 14), allowing at least 2 inches
of space between the numerals. Tape one sheet of stencil paper over the
border design and the other over the numerals. Using the X-acto knife, cut
out each of the stencil designs. Then cut around each of the designs,
leaving at least a 1-inch border all around.

2.   Make sure that the surface you have chosen to stencil is clean, dry,
and free from wax, grease, or oil. Then determine exactly where and in
what direction you want to stencil the hopscotch. Using the yardstick and
the chalk, draw a guideline that is 10 feet long. Position the large stencil
near one end of the line, making sure that the guideline runs directly
through the middle of the stencil, as shown.

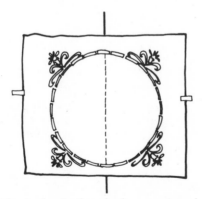

The guideline will help to keep the design centered as you repeat the
stencil. Tape the stencil in place.

3.   Squeeze a small amount of red paint onto a paper plate. Dip the tip of
the #8 stencil brush into the paint, and remove the excess paint by pouncing the brush on some newspaper. Keeping the edges of the stencil
openings pressed down with your fingers as you stencil, apply the color
through the stencil openings. When all the openings have been coated

Each square = 1 inch

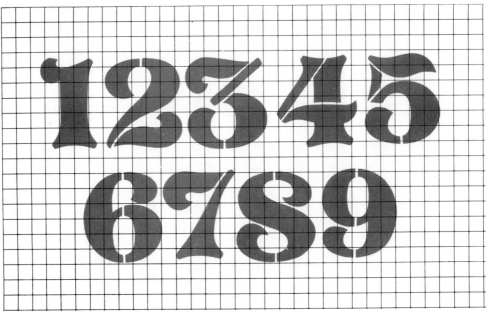

Each square = 1 inch

with a thin layer of paint, carefully remove the stencil and let the design set for a moment until it is dry to the touch.

4. To complete the body of the hopscotch, you will need to repeat the process described in steps 2 and 3 a total of eight more times until the hopscotch looks like this.

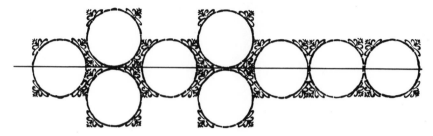

As you position the stencil each time, make sure that you use the guideline to center it. Also make sure that the openings of the stencil almost touch the lower edge of the design that you have previously stenciled. When all nine circular designs have been stenciled, wash the brush and set aside the stencil; you are now ready to stencil the numerals.

5. Center each of the numerals in the appropriate box, as shown in the illustration, and tape them in place.

Using a #12 brush and the sky blue paint, stencil the 1 and the 4, following the stenciling procedure described in step 3. Using a clean, dry #12 brush and the bright pink paint, stencil the 2 and the 7. With the green paint and another #12 brush, stencil the 3 and the 9. Stencil the 5 with the orange paint and another clean, dry #12 stencil brush. Do the 6 with the purple paint and another clean, dry #12 brush. Finally, do the 8 with the cobalt blue and a #12 brush. When all the numerals have been stenciled, remove the stencils and allow the hopscotch to dry for 24 hours.

Hints and Ideas:

★If you wish your hopscotch to be really permanent, use outdoor enamel paint or deck paint. For less permanence than the acrylics provide for, use poster paint, which will wash off with water. You can also use japan colors or spray paint to stencil the designs. If you use spray paint, leave a wide margin around each design and weight down the stencils with small rocks.

★If you'd like to stencil this project on a wooden floor in the house, use the same materials called for in the stenciled Early American Hardwood Floor project on page 149.

Colonial Coal Scuttle

When our assistant artist Marty first came East from southern California, he was totally unprepared for winter's icy blasts. In memory of his first New York winter, which he spent huddled beside a coal-burning fireplace in a small, drafty apartment, we've included a design for a coal scuttle.

Our design is an Americana harvest stencil; this adaptation of folk-art motifs has been handled with a special stenciling technique that makes it possible to stencil designs that appear to be antique. If you don't have a coal-burning fireplace, a stenciled coal scuttle can become a charming accessory almost anywhere in your home. Use it as a planter, a magazine caddy, or an ice bucket.

Materials:

coal scuttle
1 piece illustration board, 15 by 20 inches
scissors
1 sheet stencil paper, 18 by 24 inches
masking tape
#1 X-acto knife with #11 blades
newspaper
nonpermanent spray adhesive
acrylic tube paints, in red, yellow ochre, moss green, and medium blue
paper plates
4 stencil brushes, all #1
rubber cement thinner
paper towels

Procedure:

1.   This project involves the early American stenciling technique of highlighting and shading. There are several ways of approaching this technique,
all of which are described in Chapter 1, page 25. Be sure to read this
section and then to practice each method. Once you have mastered the
technique, you will find that you can improve any stenciled design with
highlights and shadows. The eye does not always know why it prefers one
design over another, but it is often because of this sort of subtle shading.

Each square = 1 inch

2.   Even though this project requires a four-color stenciling process, you
can achieve beautiful results with only one stencil. Enlarge the design to
size on the illustration board (see page 14). Trim the stencil paper slightly
smaller than the illustration board and tape it in place over the design.
Using the X-acto knife, cut the stencil and then cut around the stencil on
the dotted line. The unusual shape of the outline of the stencil is necessary
in order for it to conform to the contours of the scuttle.

3.   Spread a layer of newspaper on top of your work surface and lay the
stencil, wrong side up, on top. Then lightly spray the back side of the

stencil with the adhesive and let it dry until just slightly sticky. Position the stencil on the scuttle as shown, sticky side against the scuttle, and gently press down the edges with your fingers.

4.   Squeeze a small amount of red paint onto a paper plate, dip the tip of a stencil brush into the paint, and remove the excess from the brush by pouncing the bristles on some newspaper. Continue pouncing until almost all the color is removed. Then apply the paint through only the stencil openings of the flower, using an up-and-down dabbing motion and taking care not to get red paint into any of the other openings. When all the stencil openings of the flower have been coated with a thin layer of paint, dip the brush into the red paint again, remove the excess on newspaper, and apply a second coat of paint along the outside edges of the petals, as shown by the shaded areas in the illustration.

Each petal of the flower should graduate from light red to a darker red.
5.   Using the yellow ochre paint on a clean paper plate and another stencil brush, apply one even coat of yellow to only the areas shown as solid black in the illustration. Use the same stenciling technique described in step 4, and take care not to get yellow paint into any of the other stencil openings.

6. Using the green paint, a clean brush, and the same stenciling process given in step 3, apply a coat of green to the areas shown solid black or shaded in the illustration.

When you are shading, make sure you are working with a fairly dry brush so that the transition from one color to another is smooth and even.

7. Apply blue paint to the areas shown solid black or shaded in the illustration. Be sure to use a clean brush and a clean paper plate for the paint.

Clean your brushes in water and let them dry.

8. Gently remove the stencil from the scuttle. After the design has dried for 24 hours, dip paper towels into the rubber cement thinner and use them to wipe away gently all the accumulated spray adhesive. The thinner will not harm the scuttle or the acrylic paint.

Hints and Ideas:

★You can stencil this same design on the other side of the coal scuttle if you cut two stencils and turn one over for use on the reverse side.

★If you'd rather not shade your coal scuttle, simply stencil the designs with flat color.

★If you don't have a coal scuttle, stencil this design on a plain metal bucket or a metal tray.

Country Floral Wall

A summer idyll: full-bodied forests, deer glimpsed through thickets of wild grape ivy, clusters of wild blueberries and blackberries to be picked and eaten later with fresh heavy cream. Persistent wanderers may occasionally stumble upon half-ruined farmhouses submerged under fragrant masses of lilacs and honeysuckle. And it's always possible that one may chance on an even rarer surprise, a hidden meadow of day lilies, spectacular emerald-green carpets punctuated by regal white flowers.

In memory of drowsy, sun-filled days, we've brought the lilies inside and stenciled them onto a wall above a fireplace. Even in winter, when summer is a half-remembered dream, the lilies remain and seem to sway by the light of a softly crackling fire.

Materials:

smooth plaster wall,* without cracks
1 piece illustration board, 20 by 30 inches
scissors
2 sheets stencil paper, each 18 by 24 inches
masking tape
#1 X-acto knife with #11 blades
marking pen
newspaper
acrylic tube paints, in light green, light yellow, and lavender
paper plates
3 stencil brushes, all #5

*Stenciling with acrylic paints on plaster surfaces works best when the surface has been covered first with a flat latex paint. Be sure that the wall you plan to stencil is both clean and dry.

Procedure:

1.   Enlarge each of the project designs to size on the illustration board (see page 14), leaving at least 2 inches of space between the designs. Cut up the stencil paper into three sections so that two of them fit over those designs labeled A, B, C, D, and E and one over those labeled F-1, F-2, G-1, and G-2; tape the stencil paper in place to the board. Using a fresh blade in your X-acto knife, cut the stencils. Then cut around each stencil, allowing at least a 1-inch margin all around. Separate each set of stencils that you cut in duplicate and turn one of each set over to use to stencil in reverse. Arrange the stencils as shown in the illustration and label each with a piece of masking tape and a marking pen.

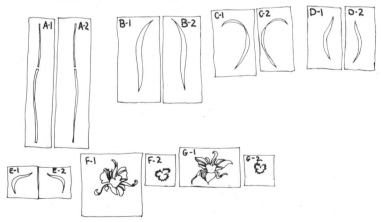

2.   Stencils A-1 and A-2 will be used to create all the stems shown in the illustration.

194

Stencil B

Stencil A

Stencil G-1

Stencil G-2

Stencil C

Stencil F-2

Stencil F-1

Stencil D

Stencil E

Each square = 1 inch

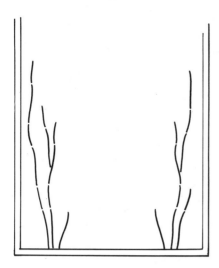

Build this stem pattern by working from the bottom up. Tape one of the stencils in place, squeeze a small amount of light green paint onto a paper plate, and dip the tip of a stencil brush into the paint. Remove the excess paint from the brush by pouncing the bristles on some newspaper. Keeping the edges of the stencil openings firmly pressed down with your fingers as you stencil, apply the paint through the openings. When all the openings have been filled with color, remove the stencils. Alternate stencils A-1 and A-2 to create the pattern shown in the above illustration.

3.   Using stencils B-1 and B-2, repeat the designs until the overall design looks like Figure A of the illustration. Follow the same stenciling procedure outlined in step 2 and use the light green paint.

Figure A

Figure B

Repeat stencils C-1 and C-2, using the same stenciling procedures given in step 2, until the design looks like Figure B of the illustration above. You should still be using the light green paint.

4.   Add more leaves by repeating stencils D-1 and D-2, again using the light green paint and the same stenciling procedure, until the design looks like Figure A of the illustration.

Figure A 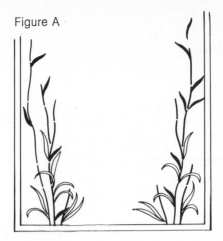 Figure B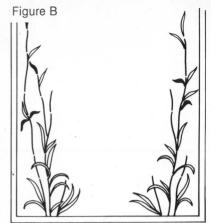

To complete the leaves, repeat stencils E-1 and E-2 until the design looks like Figure B of the illustration above. Use the light green paint.

5.   Use stencils F-1 and G-1 to stencil the flowers. Tape the stencils in place, use the light yellow paint, and choose a clean stencil brush with which to apply the design. Use the same stenciling procedure outlined in step 2, and repeat the design until the overall design looks like Figure A of the illustration.

Figure A  Figure B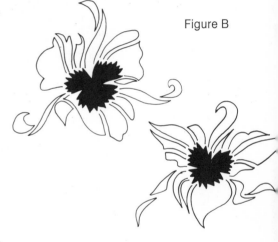

Stencils F-2 and G-2 provide the centers for the flowers, with stencil F-2 fitting into the center of stencil F-1 and stencil G-2 fitting into the center of G-1, as shown in Figure B. Tape the stencils in place; using a clean, dry brush and the lavender paint, add the centers to the flowers. Repeat the design until all the flowers have centers. Remove the stencils and allow the paint to dry.

Hints and Ideas:

★Regardless of the size of your wall, you can fill it with this design by increasing or decreasing the number of stems and flowers.

★Match the color of the flowers that you stencil to a specific color in the room; take a color swatch with you when you buy your acrylic paints.

★Use these stencils to create a border around your bedspread or curtains.

A Design Collection

ABCDEF
GHIJKLM
NOPQRS
TUVWXY
Z

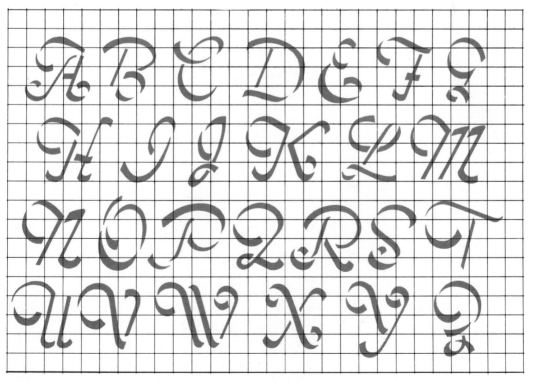

Each square = 1 inch

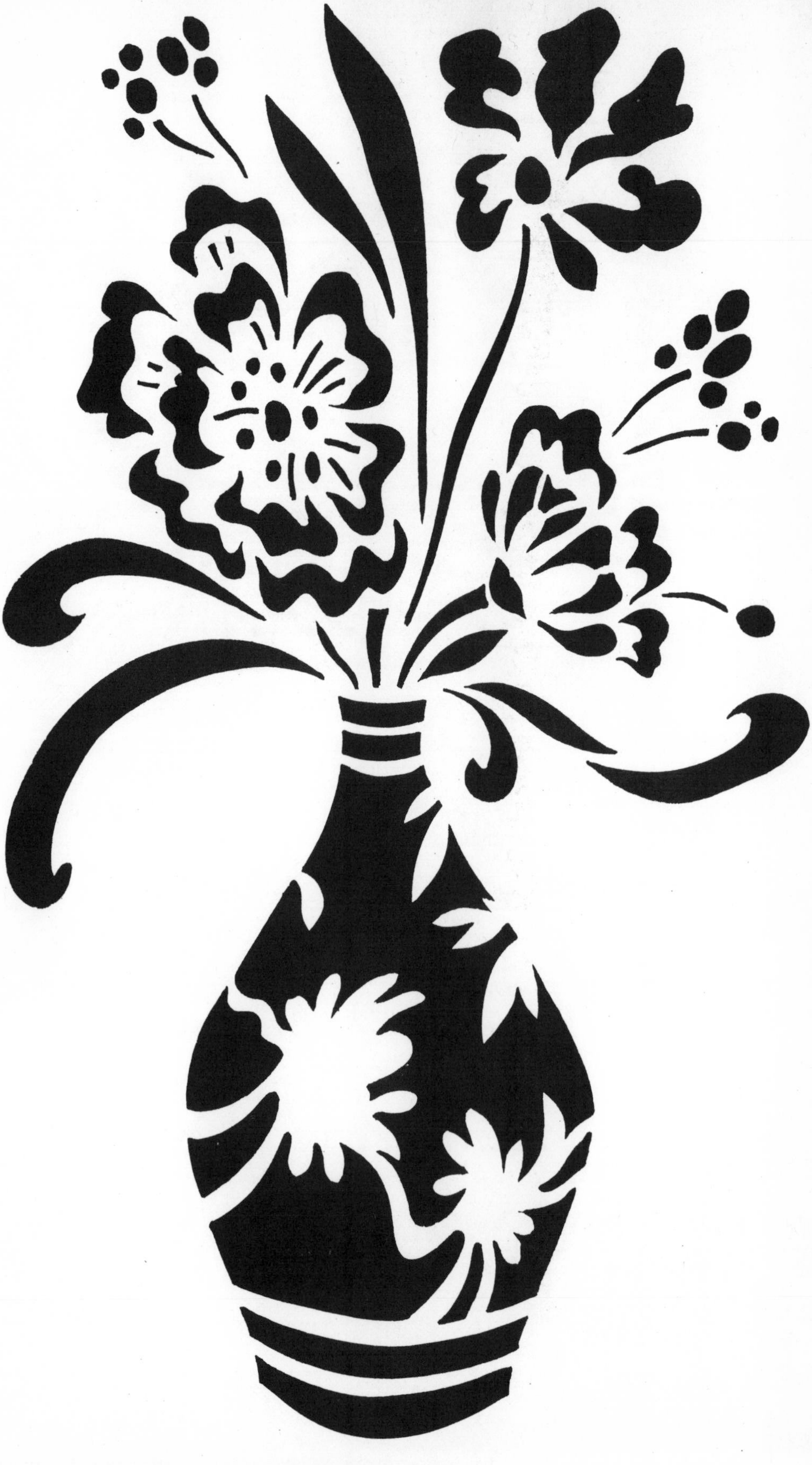